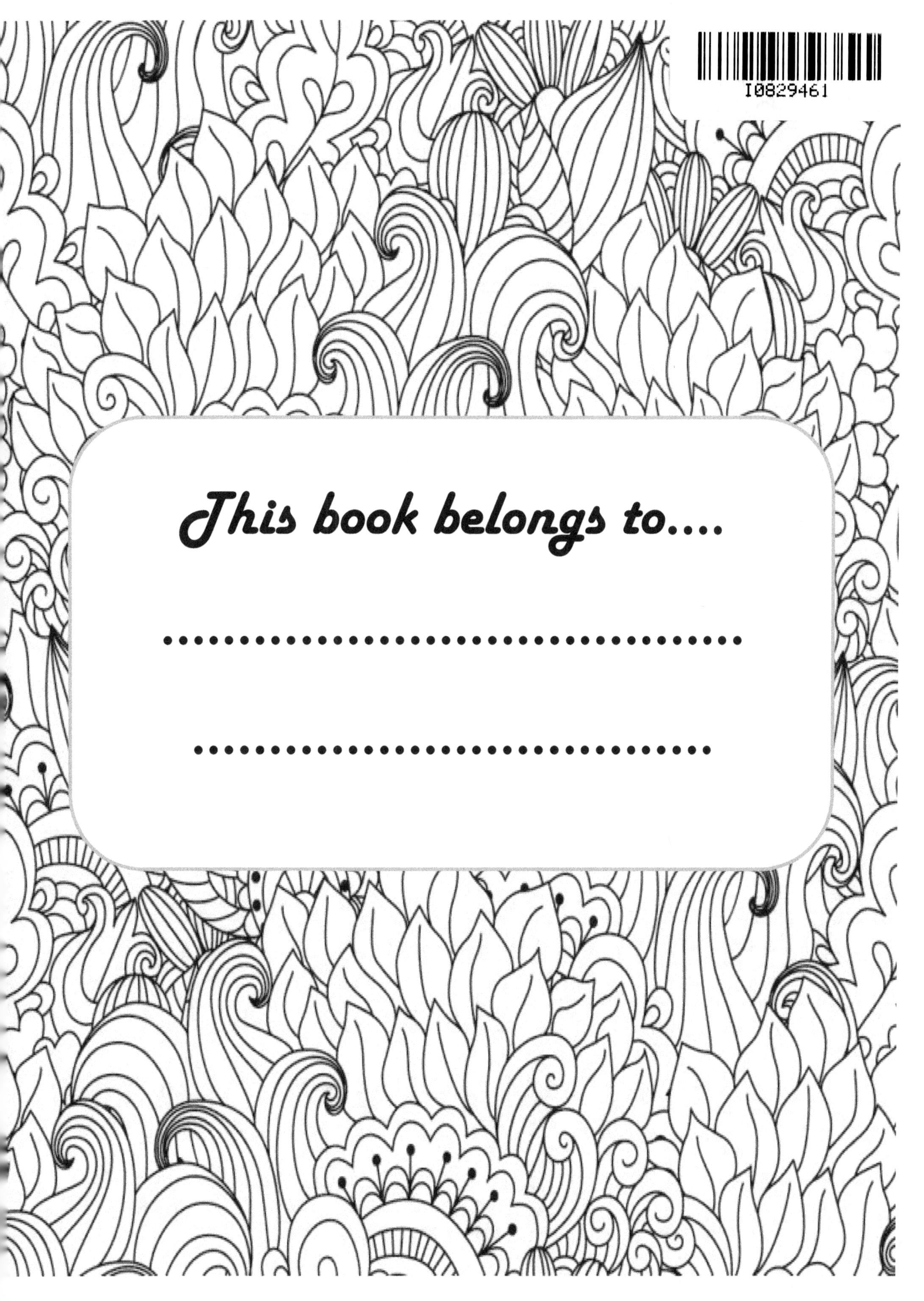

I0829461

Small preview of what's inside

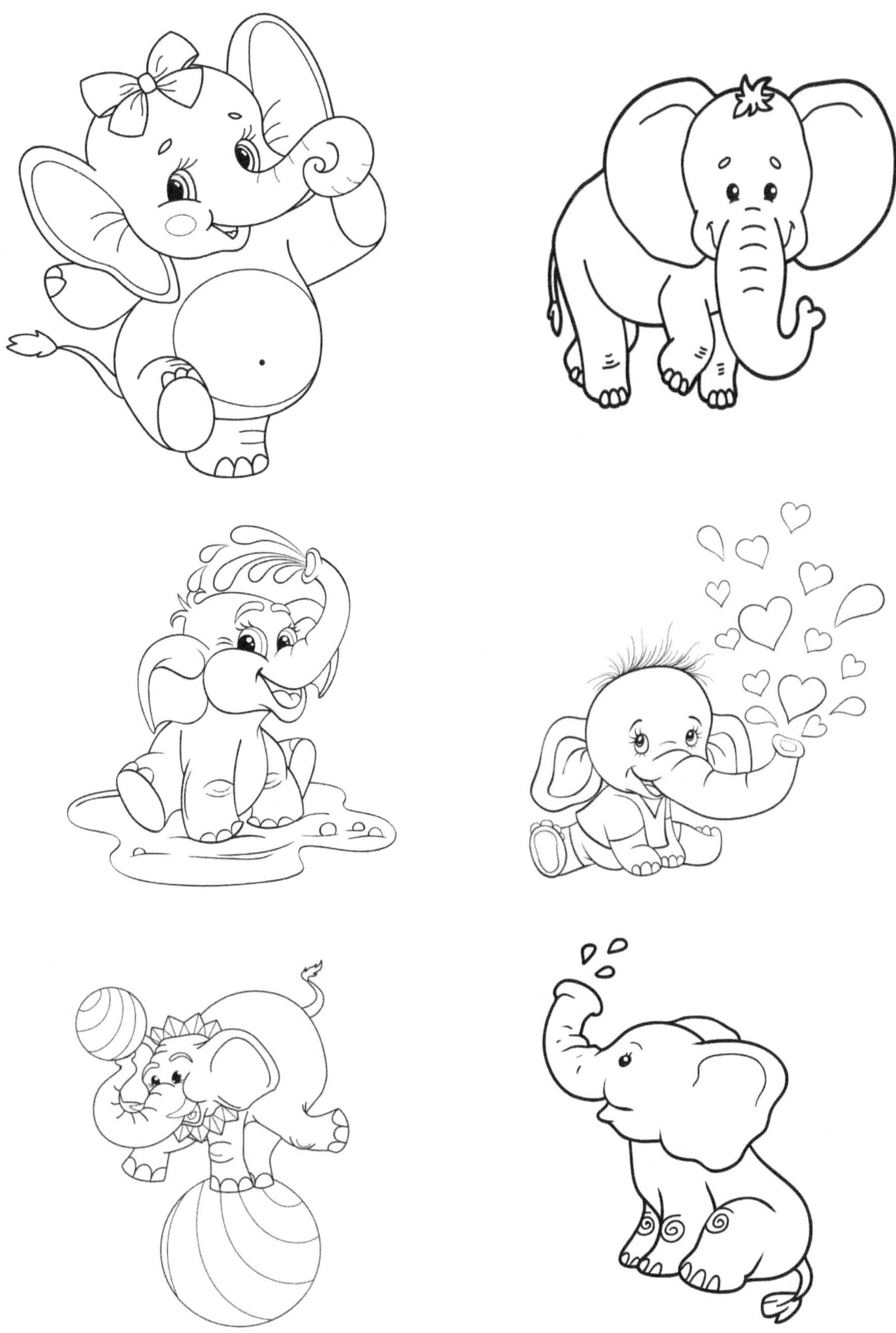

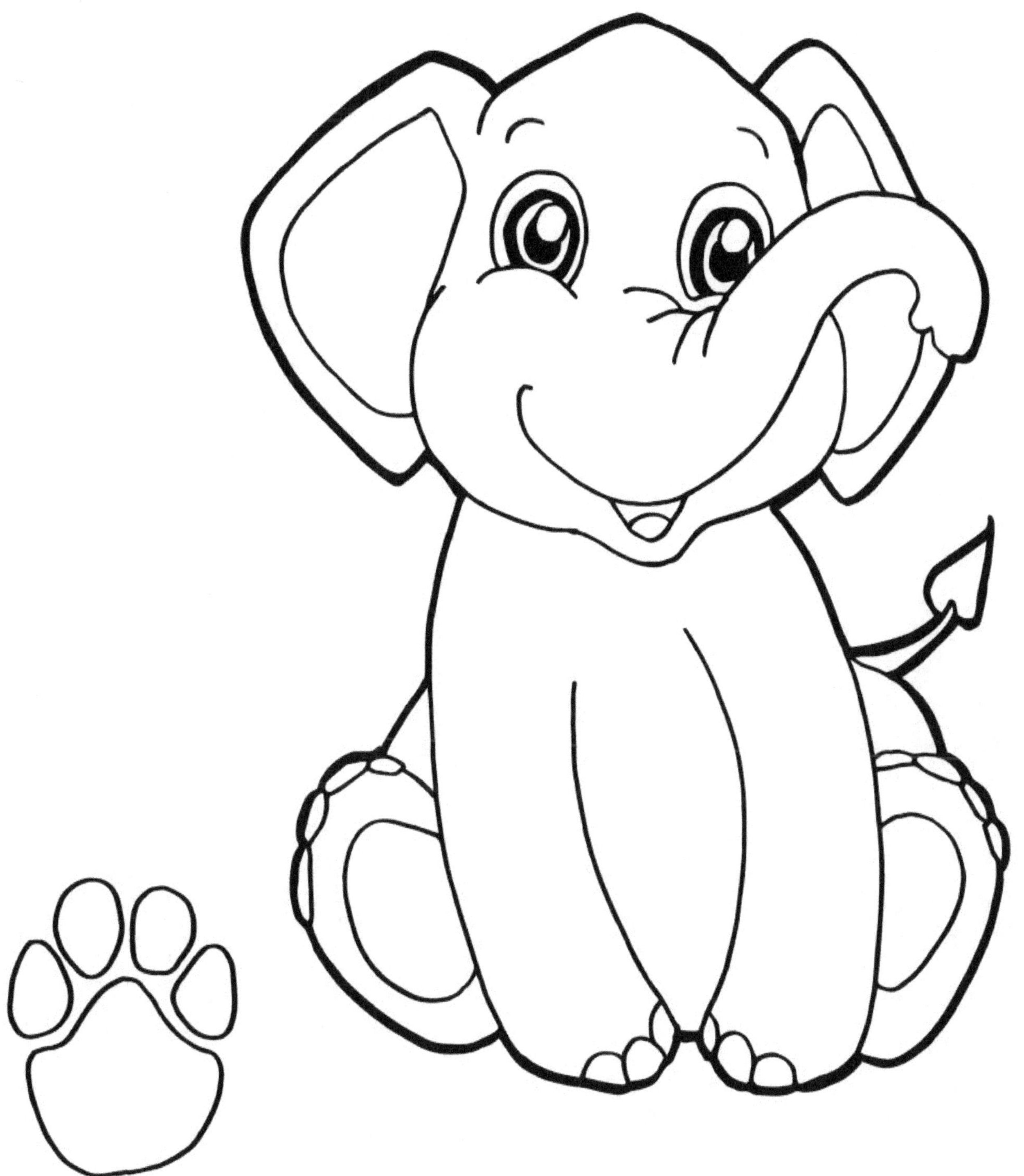

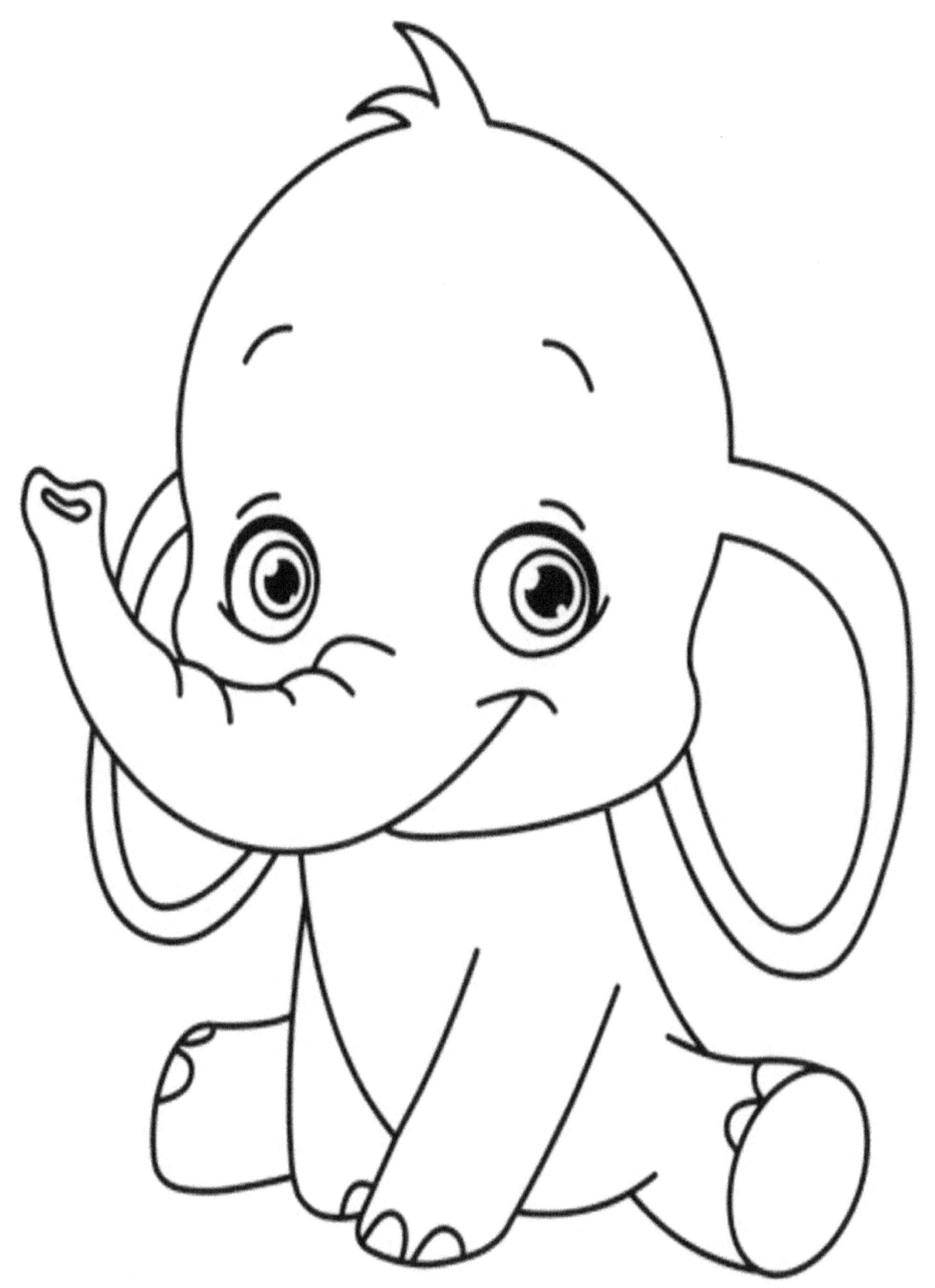

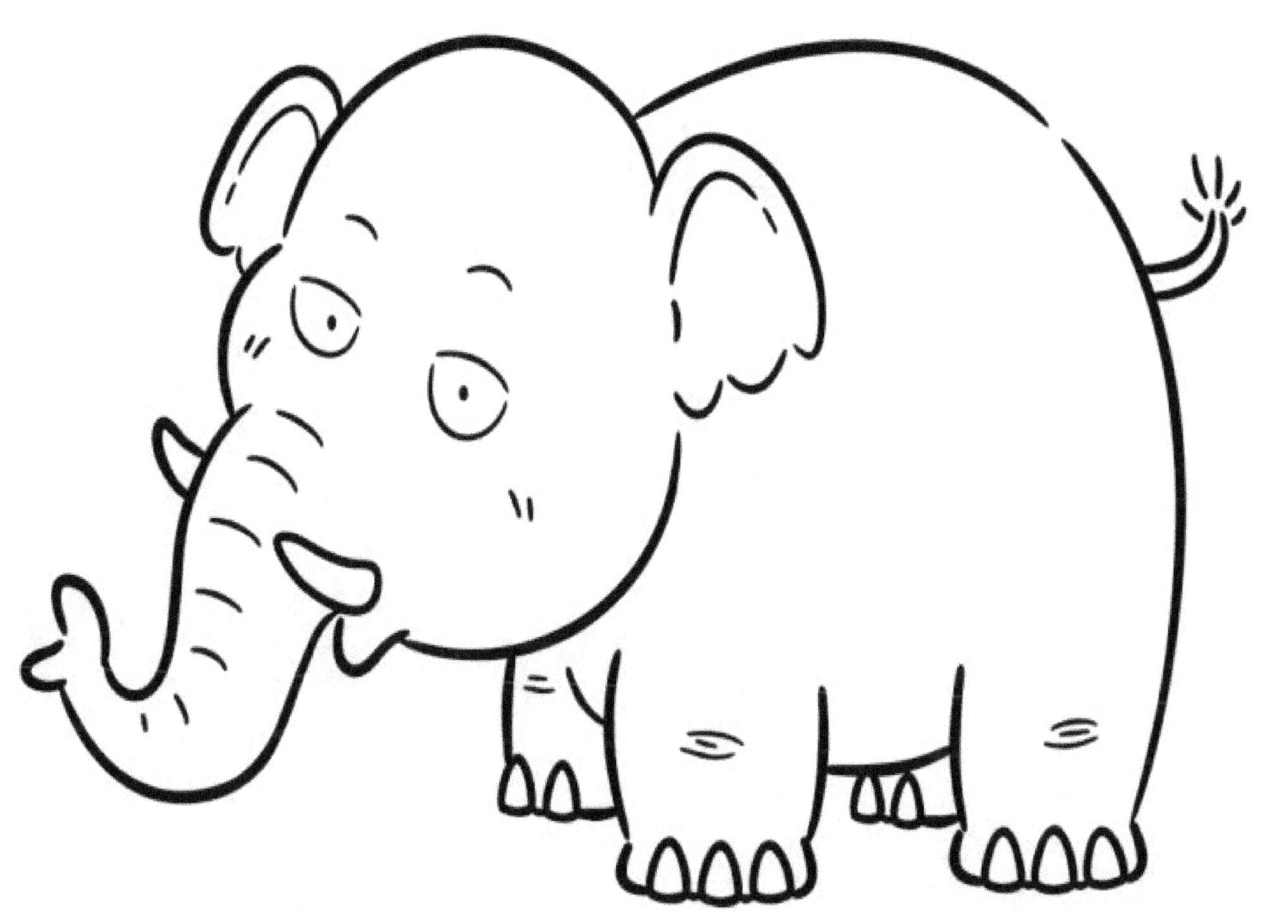

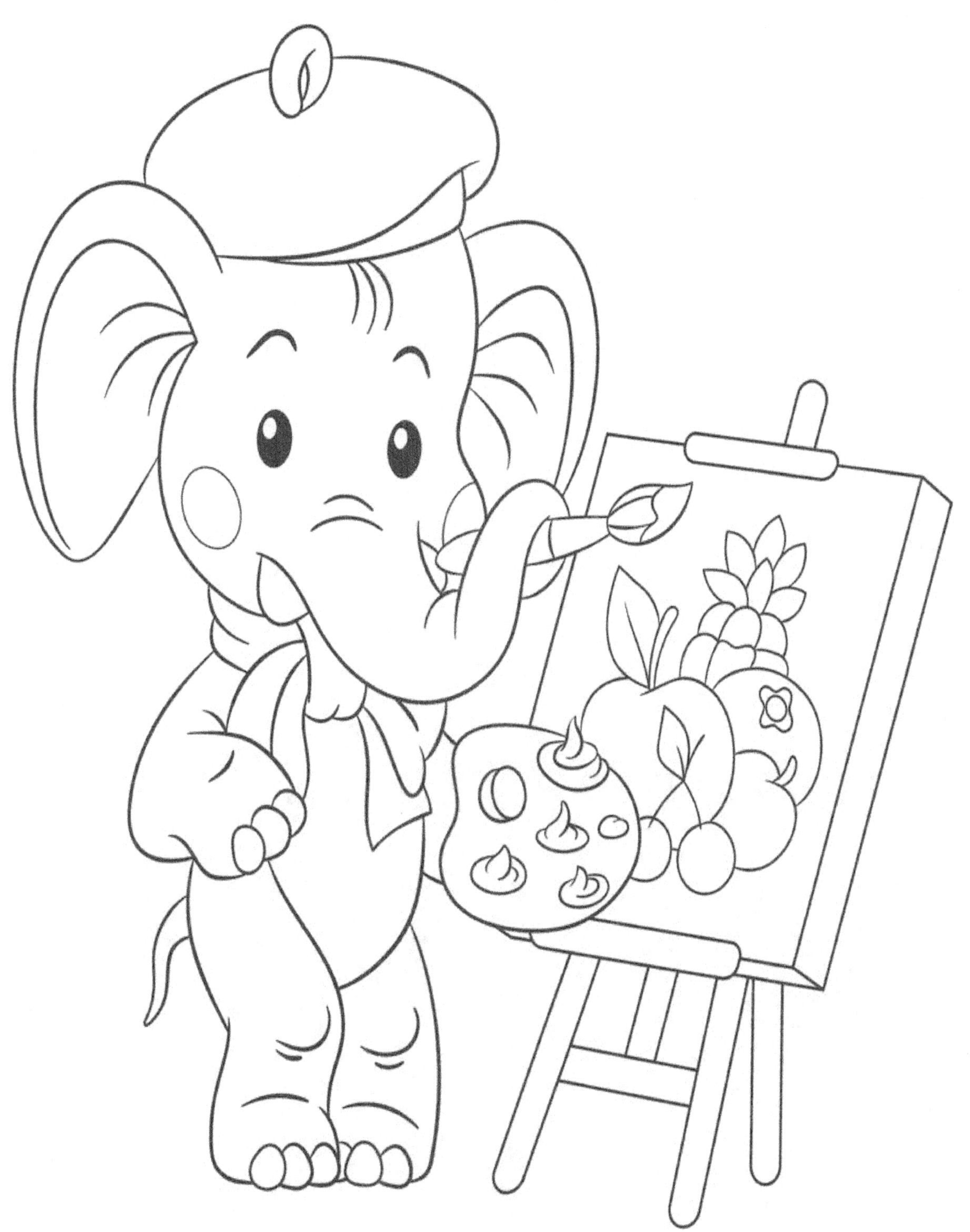

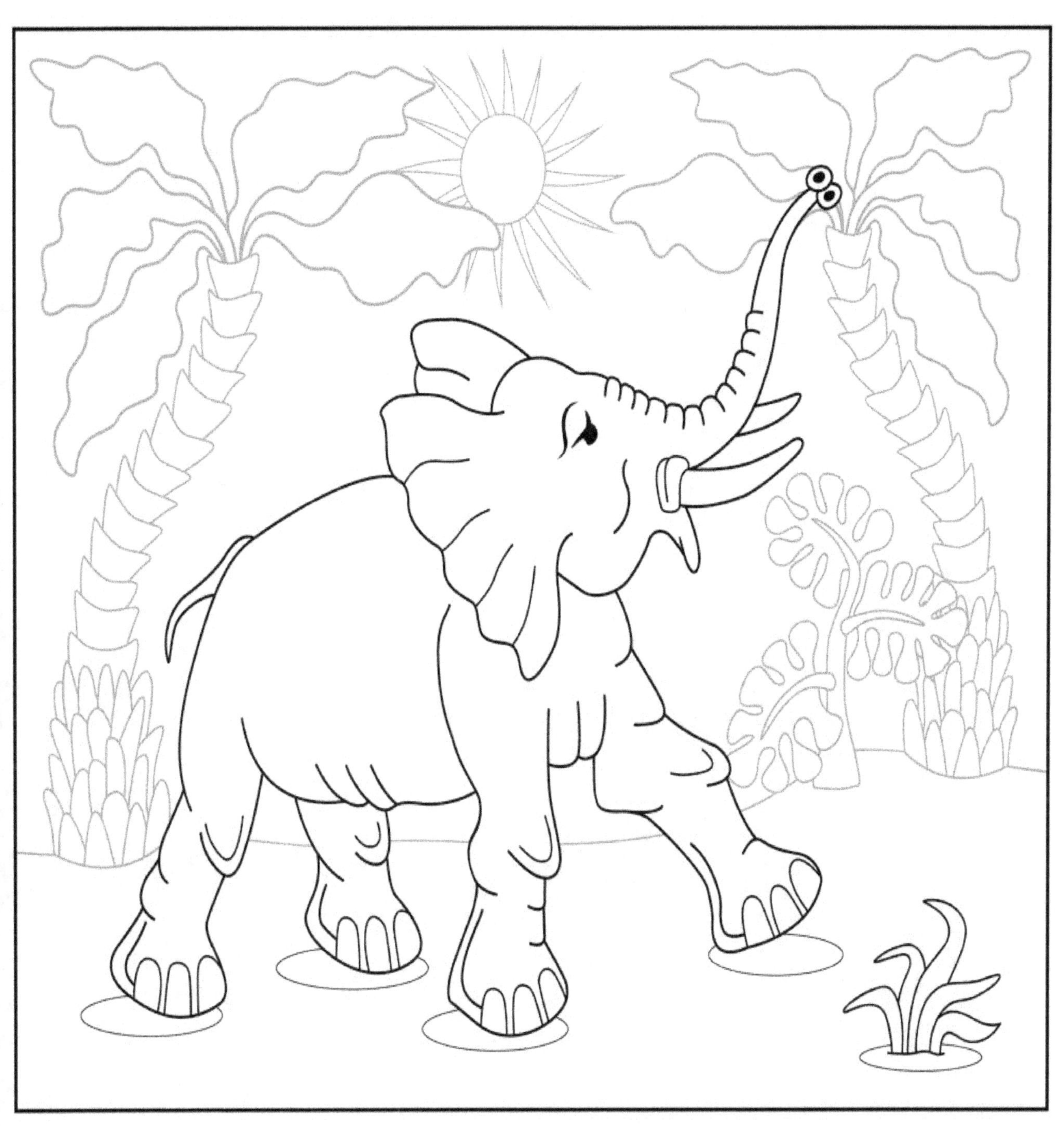

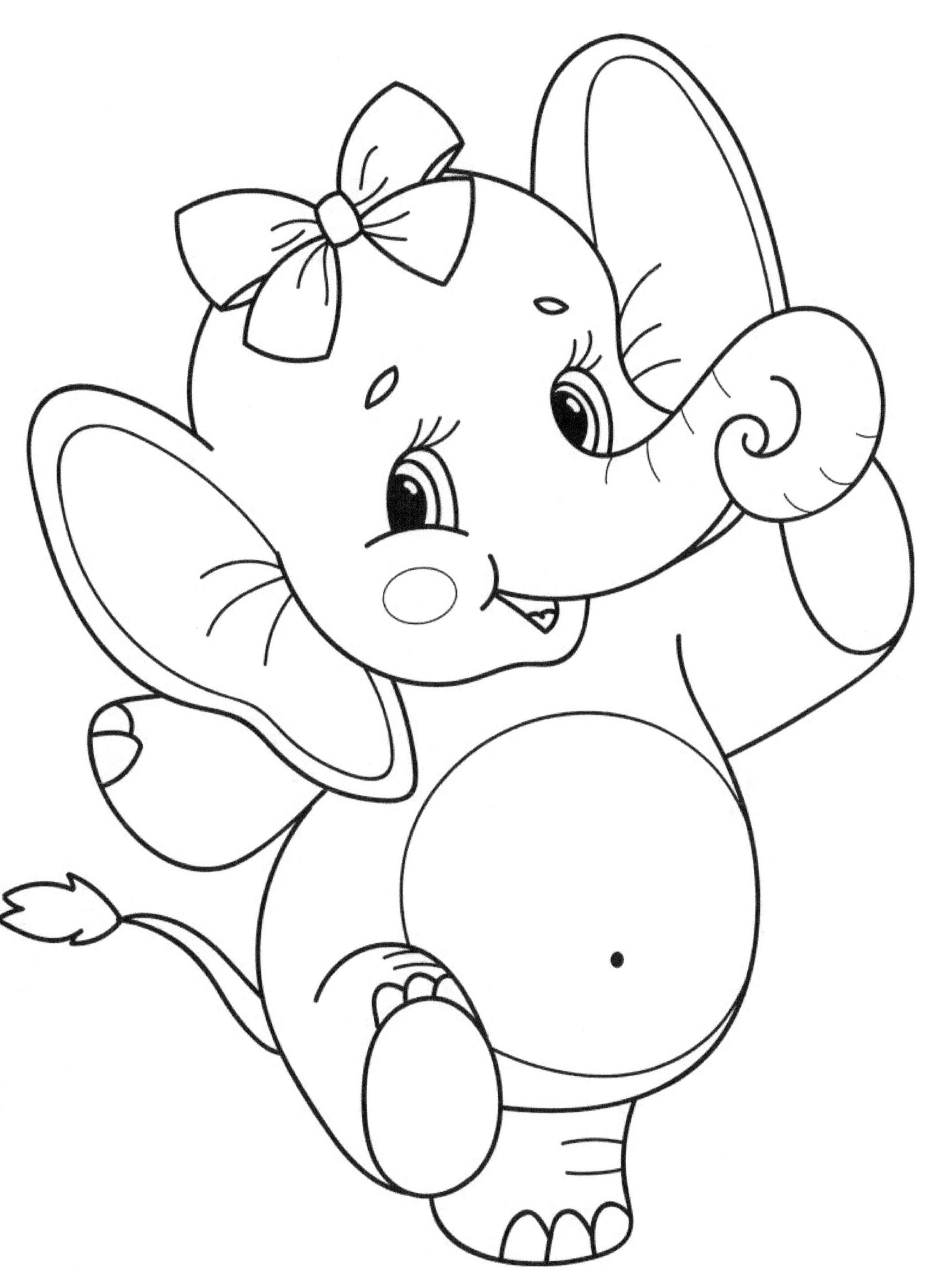

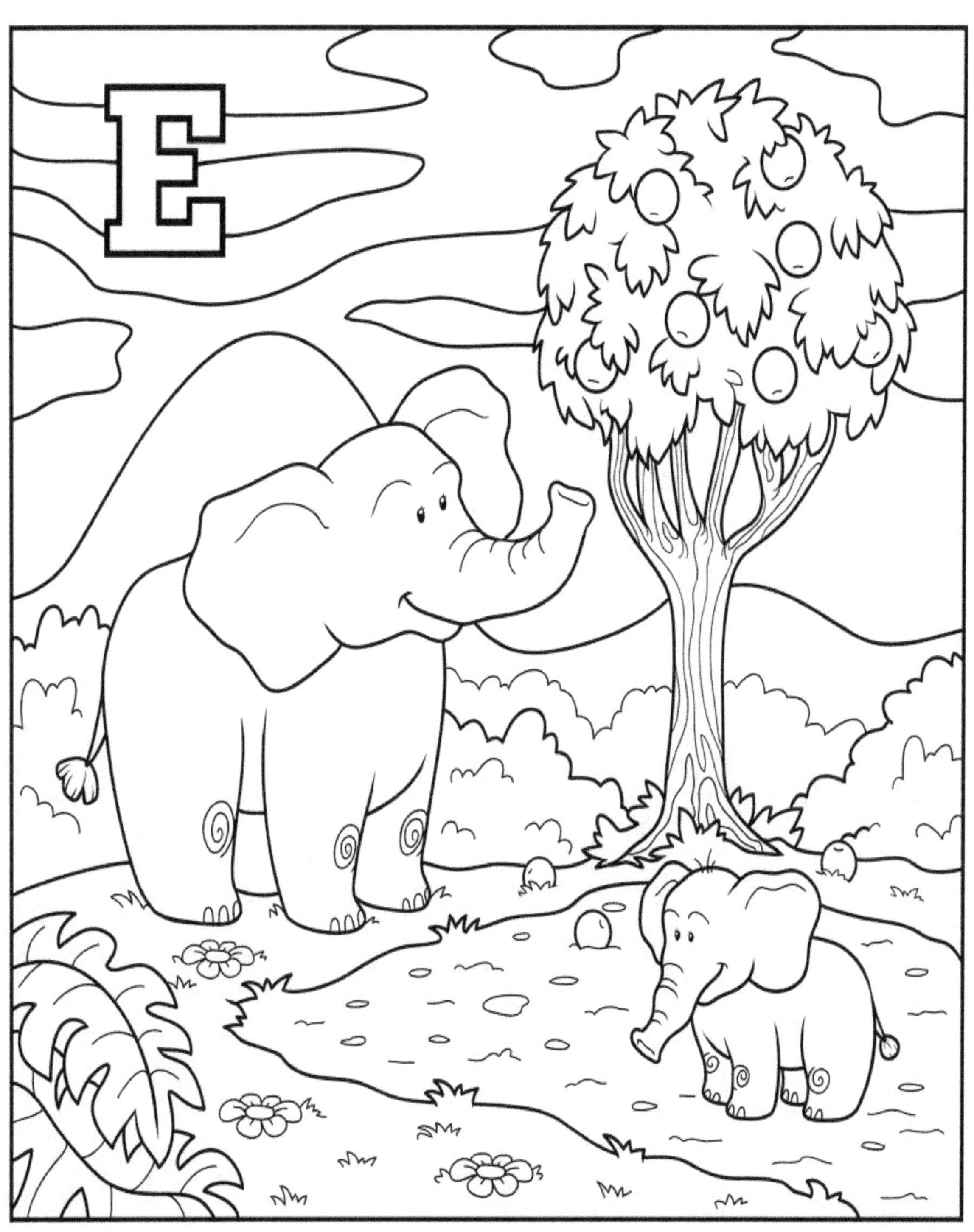

E

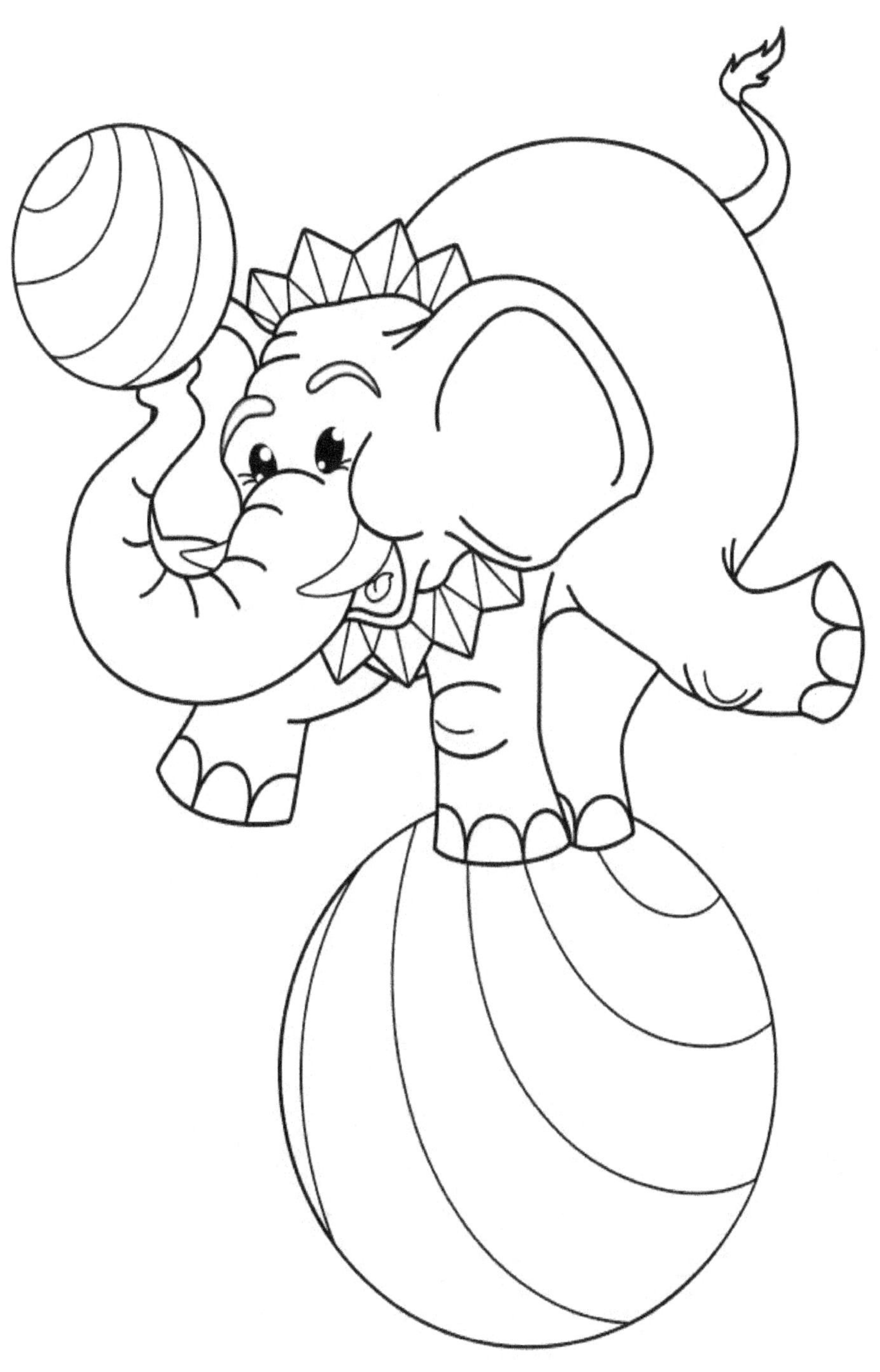

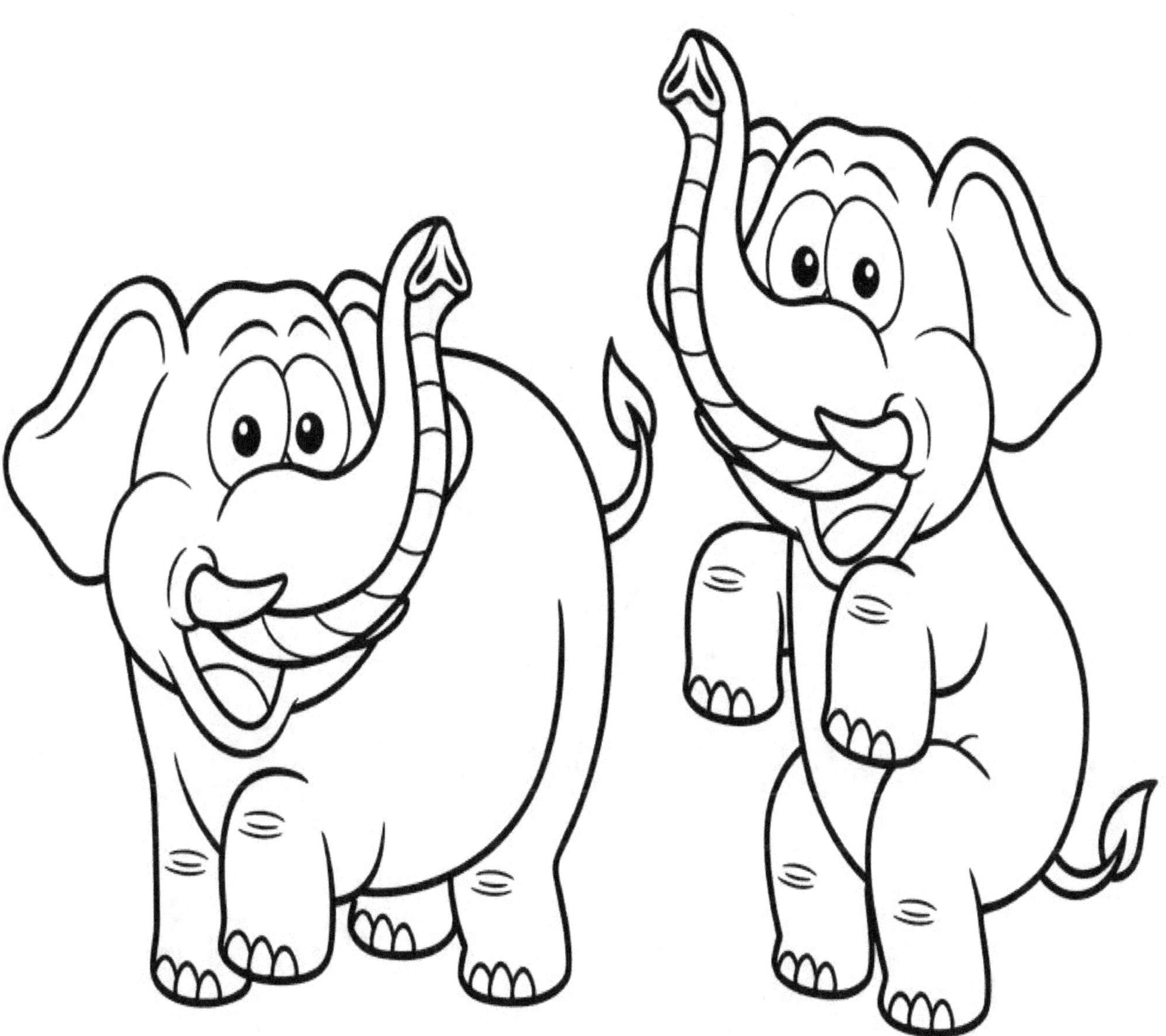

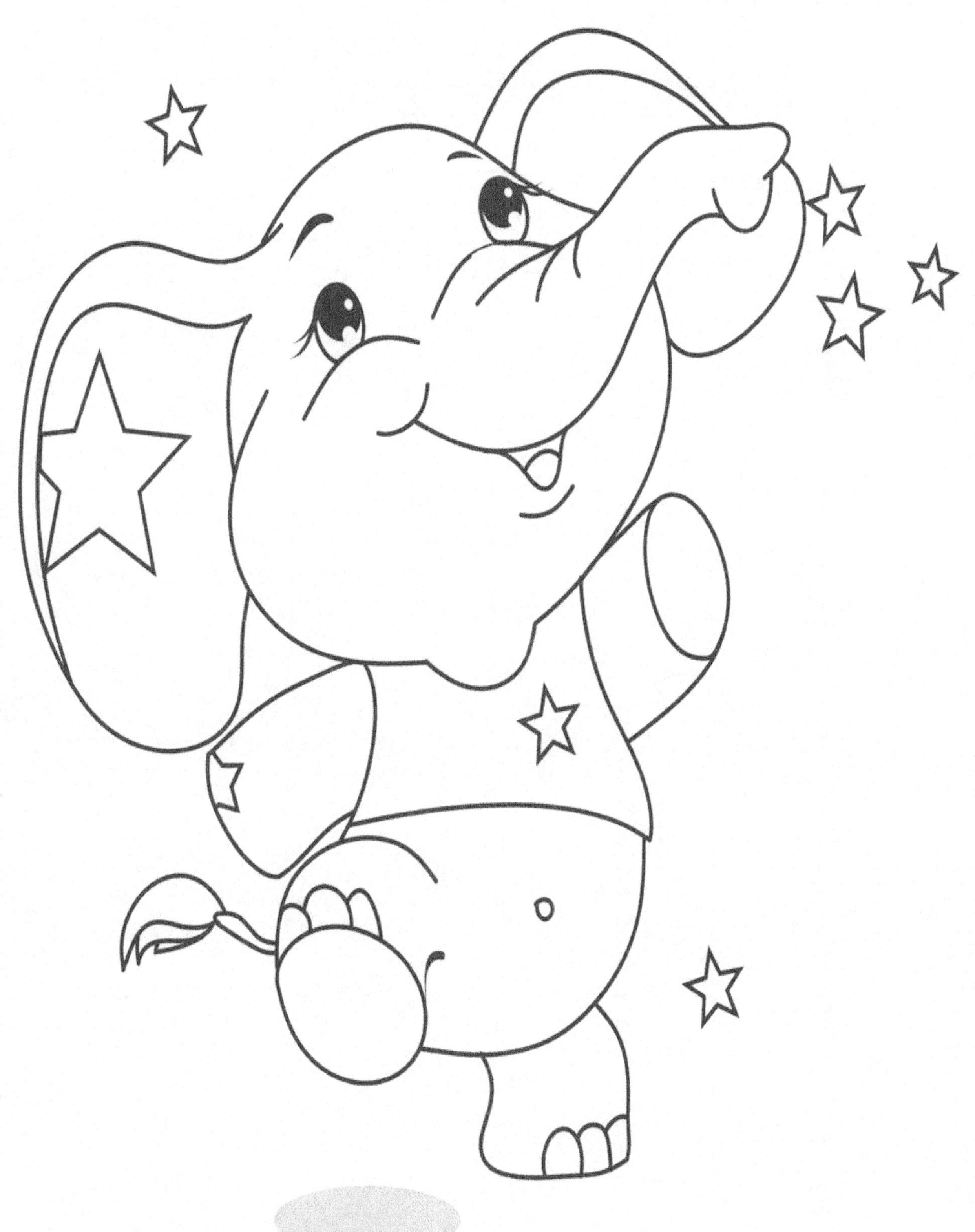

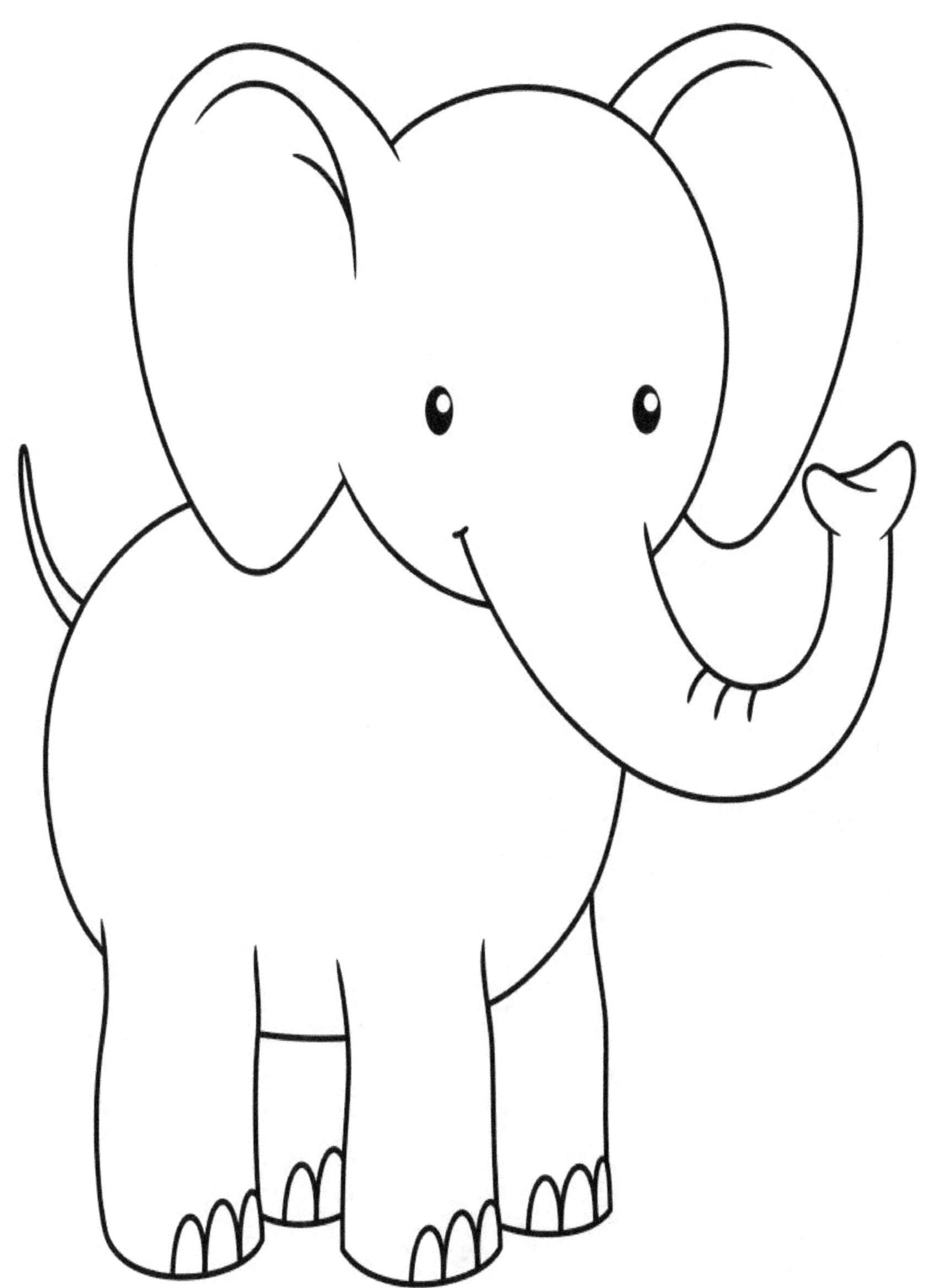

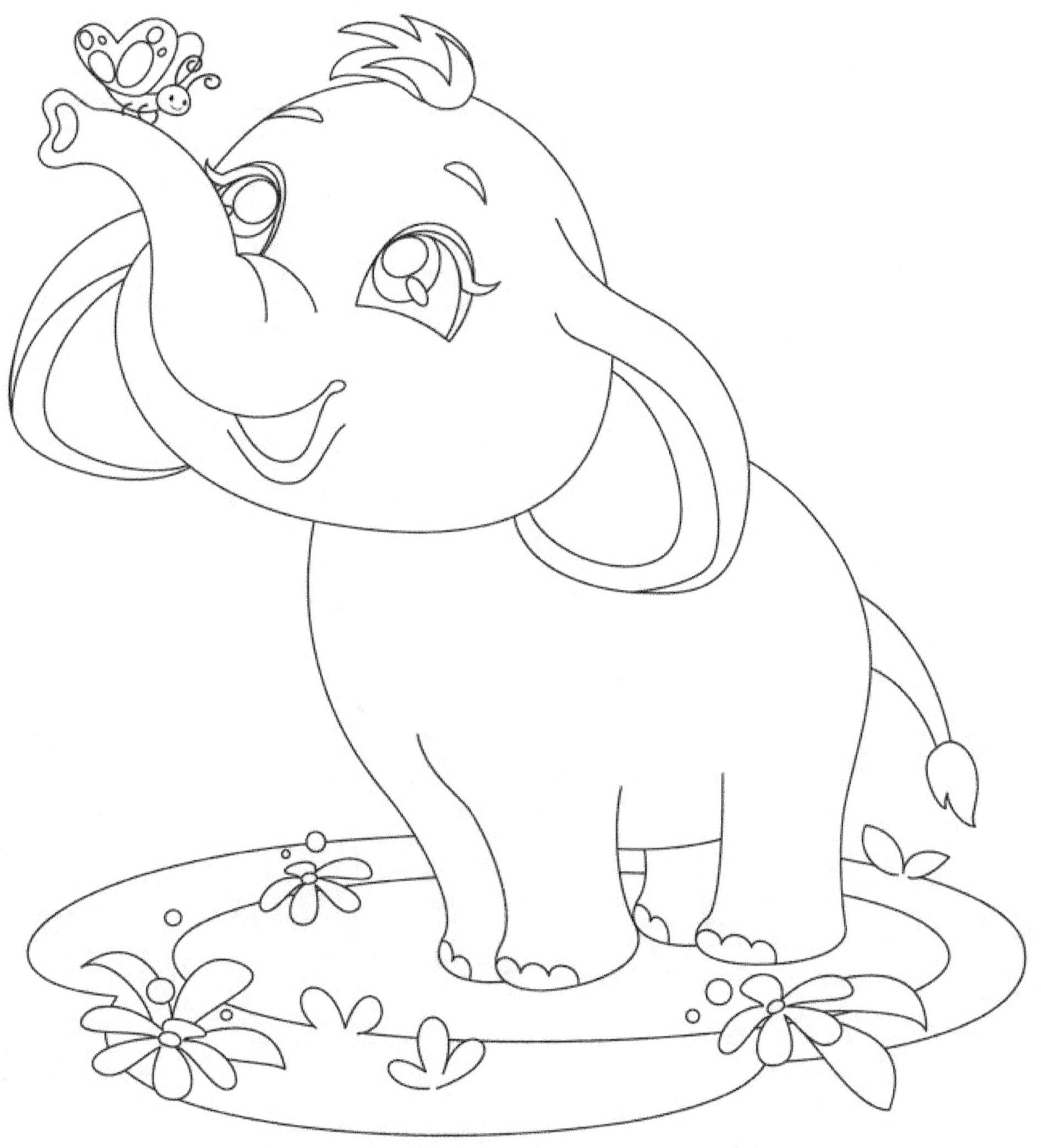

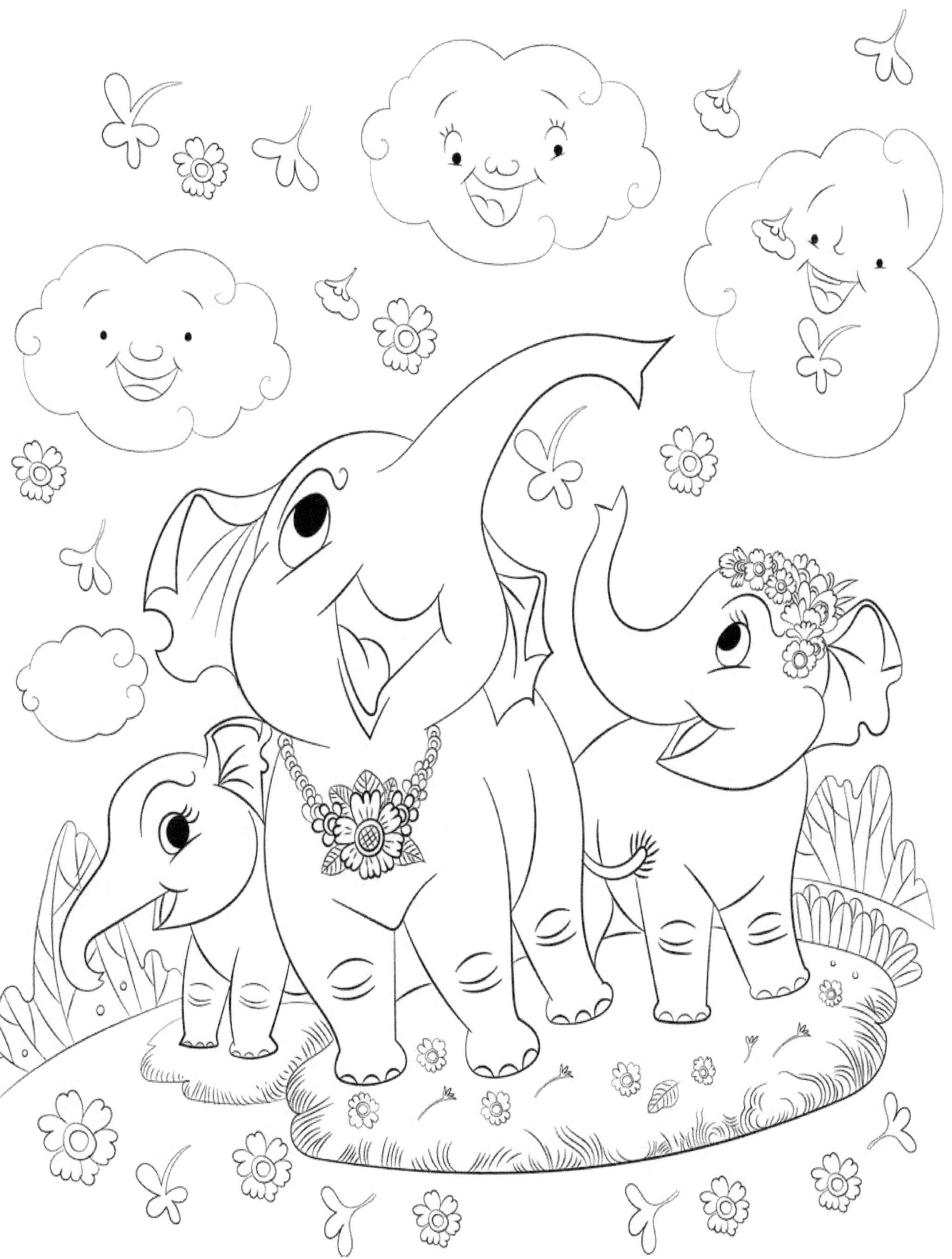

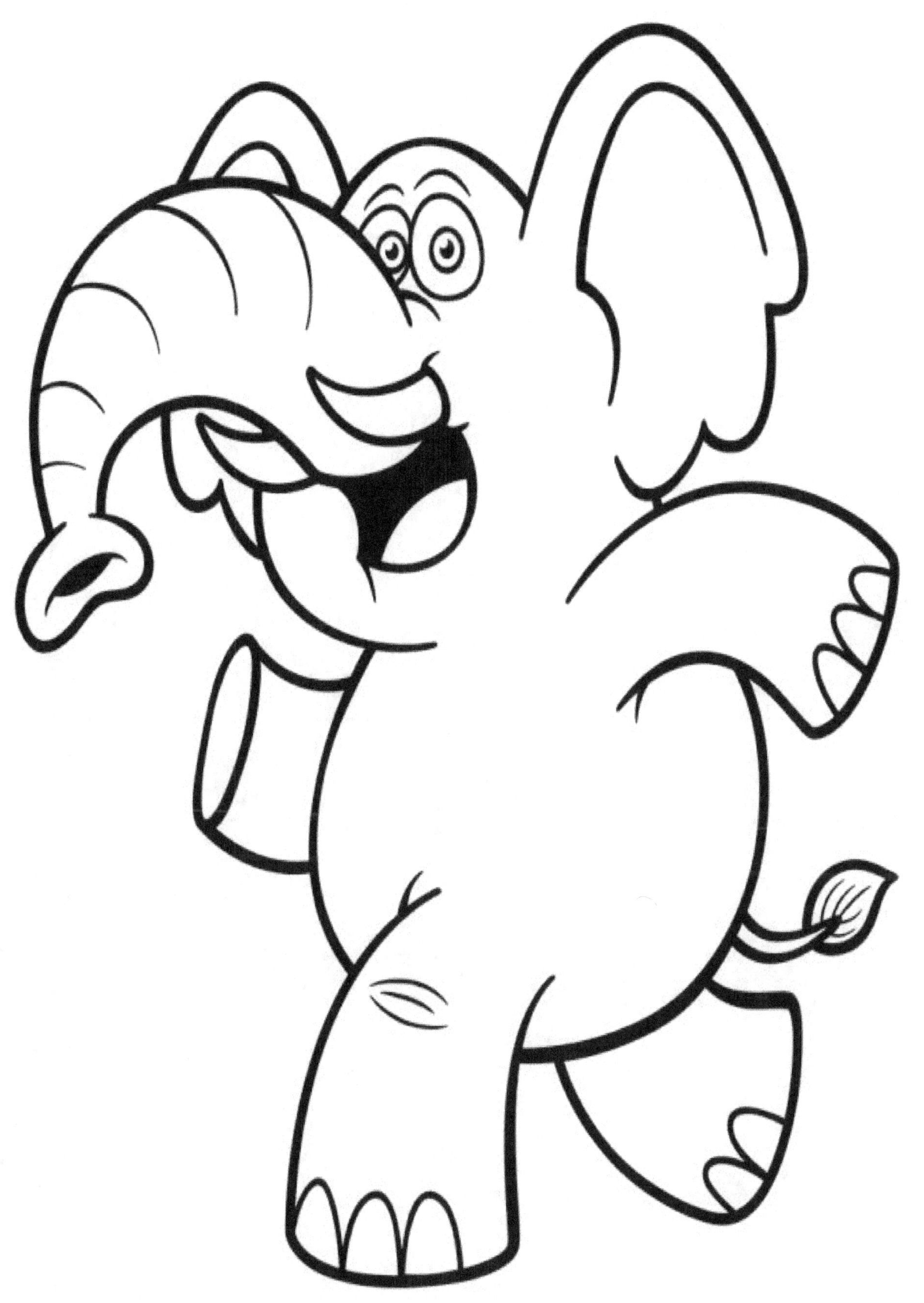

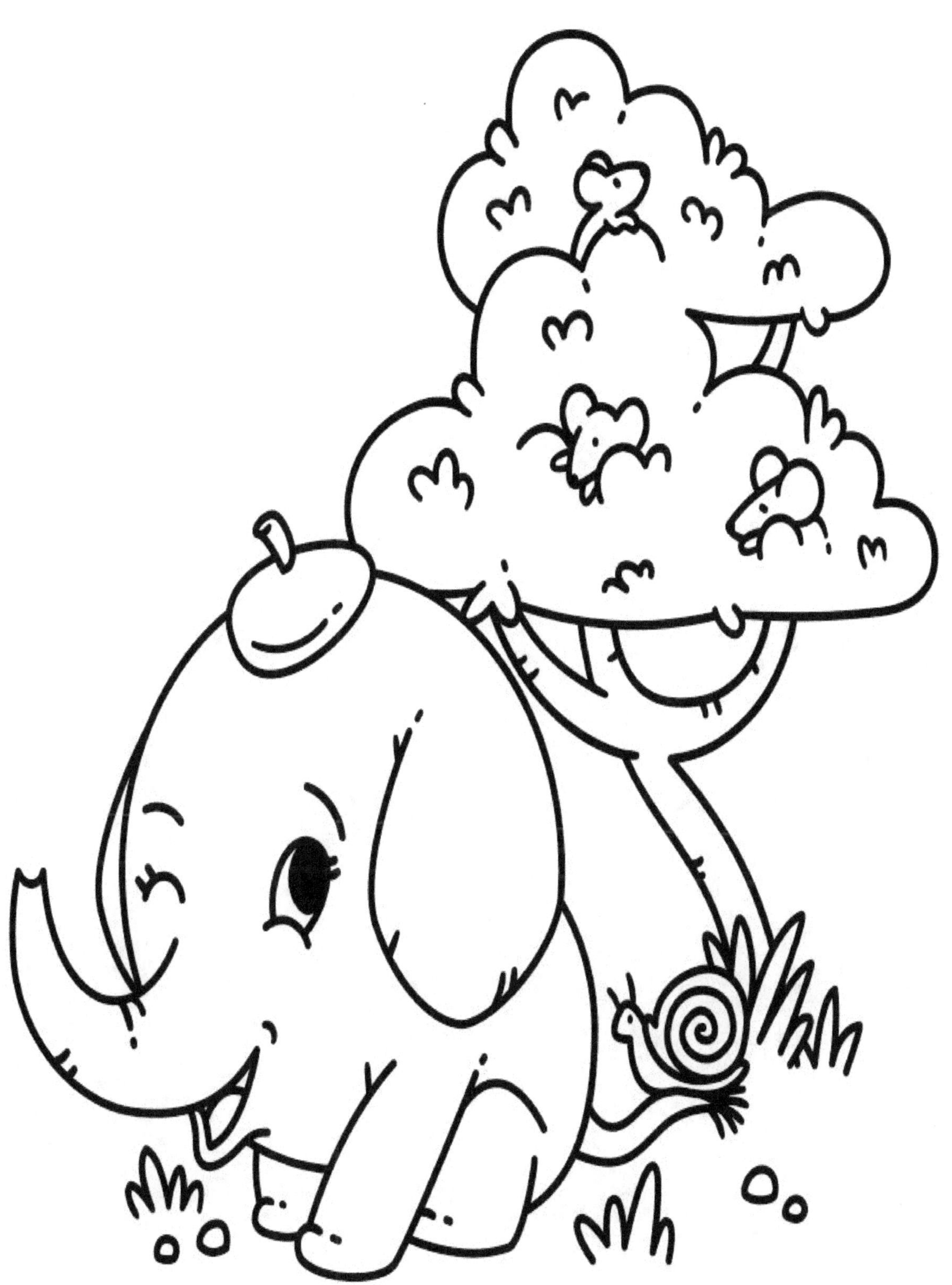

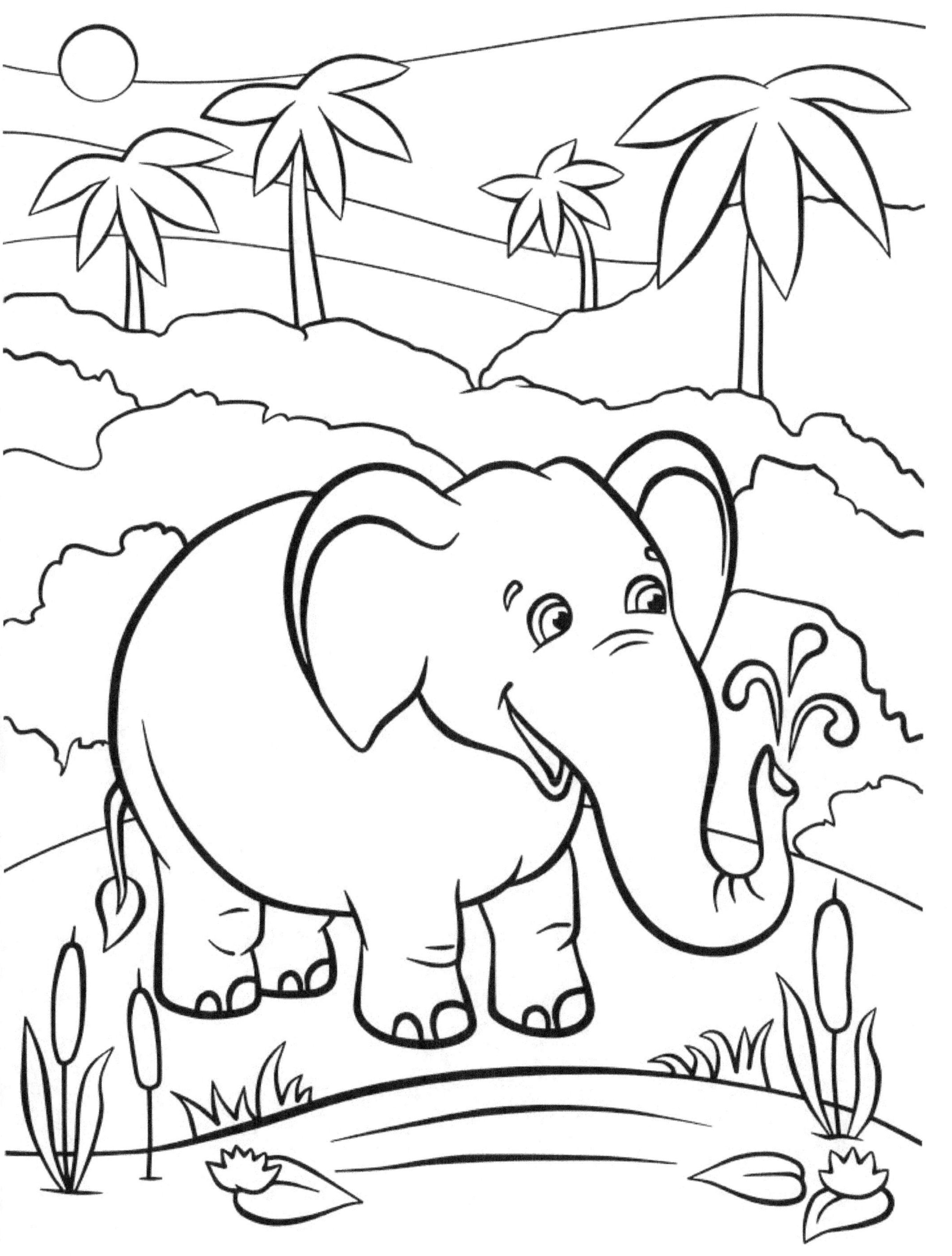

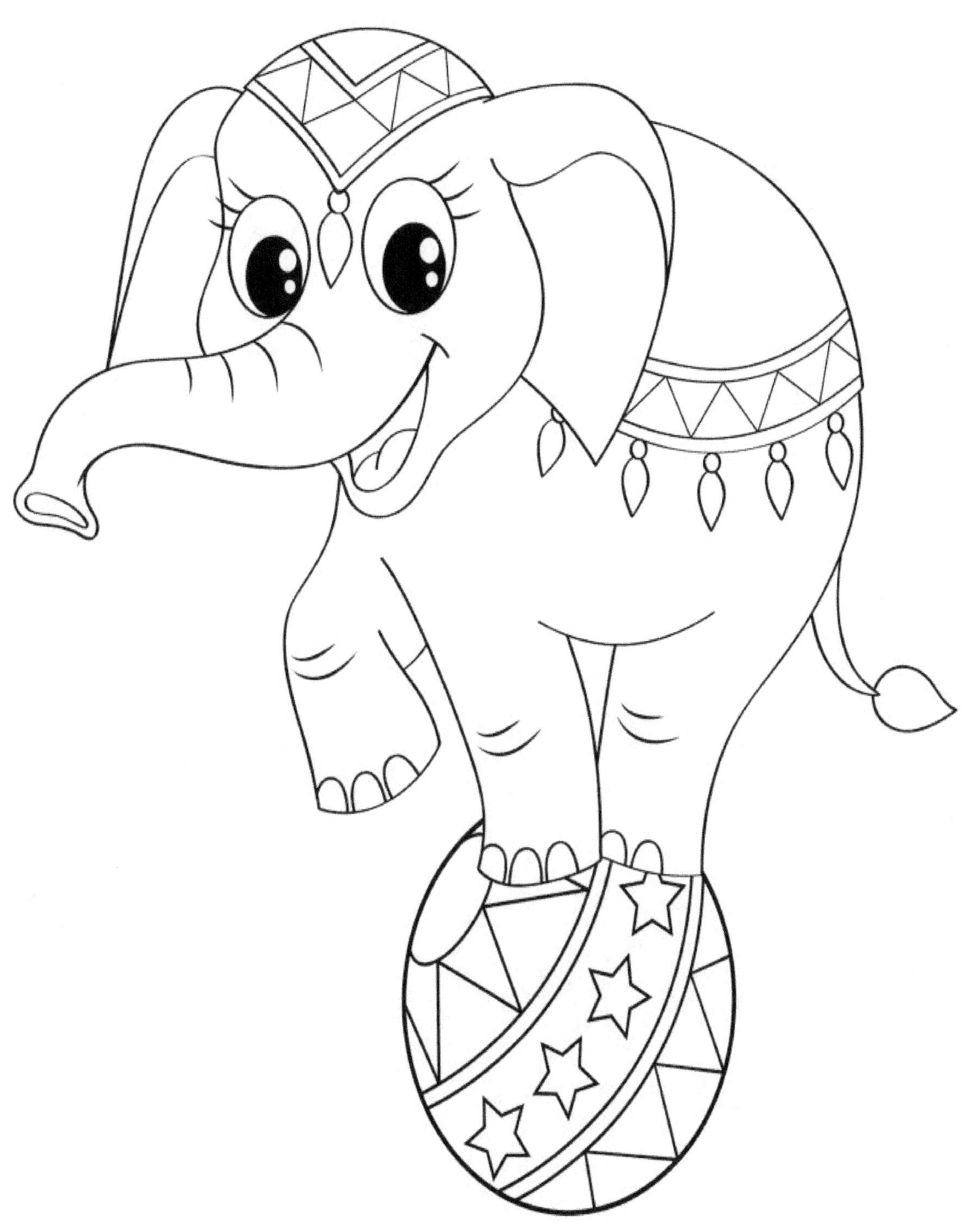

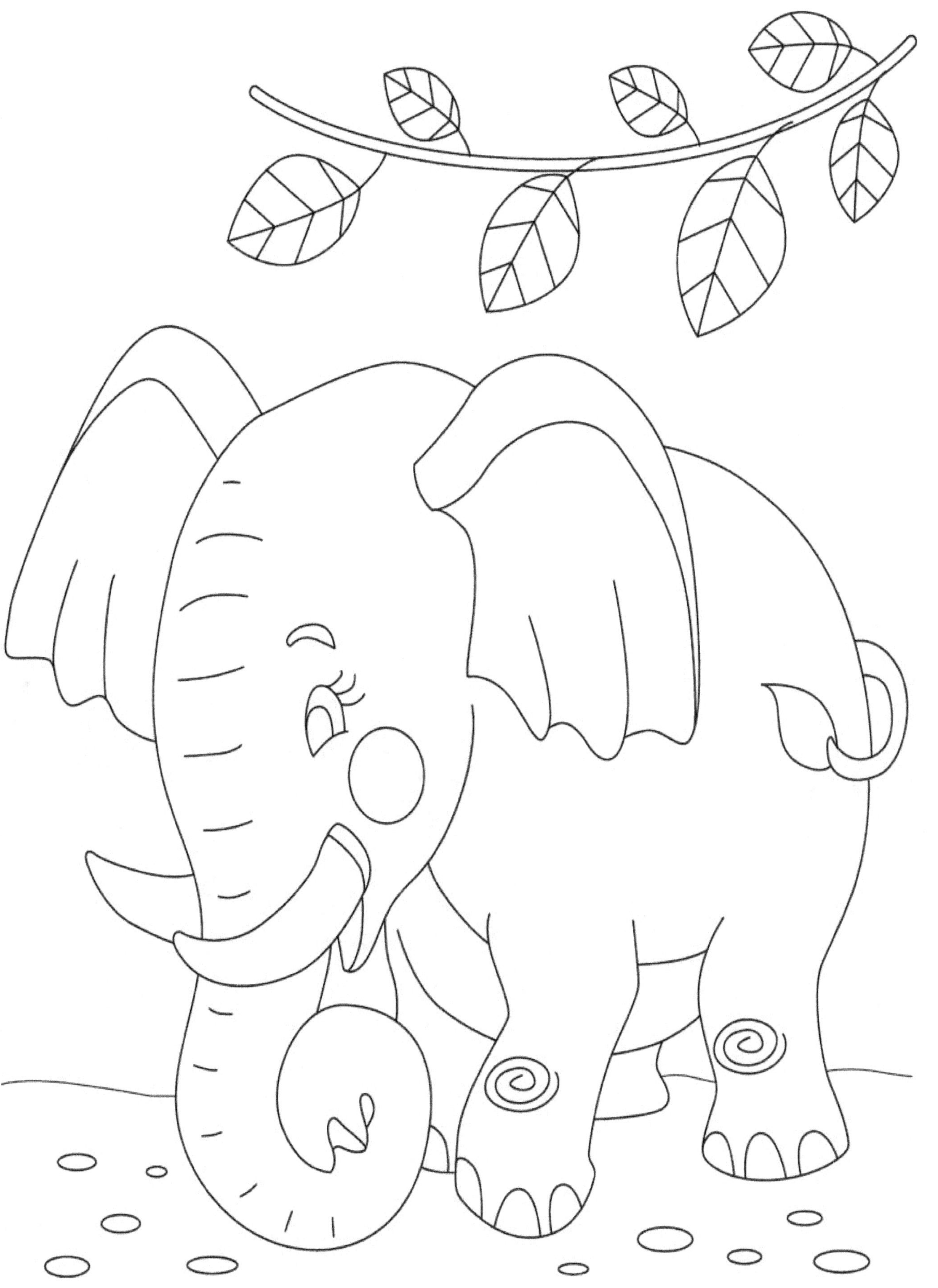

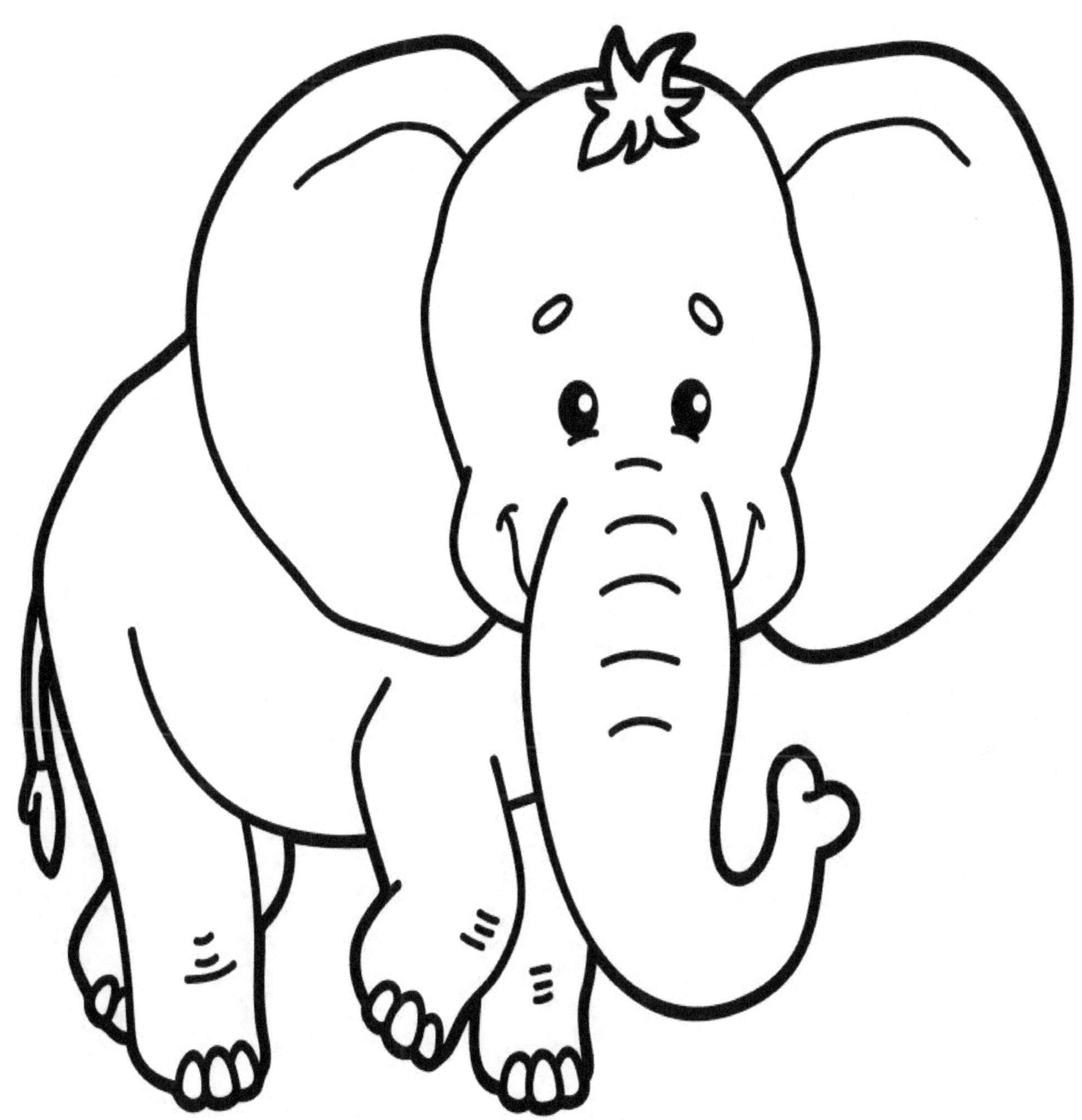

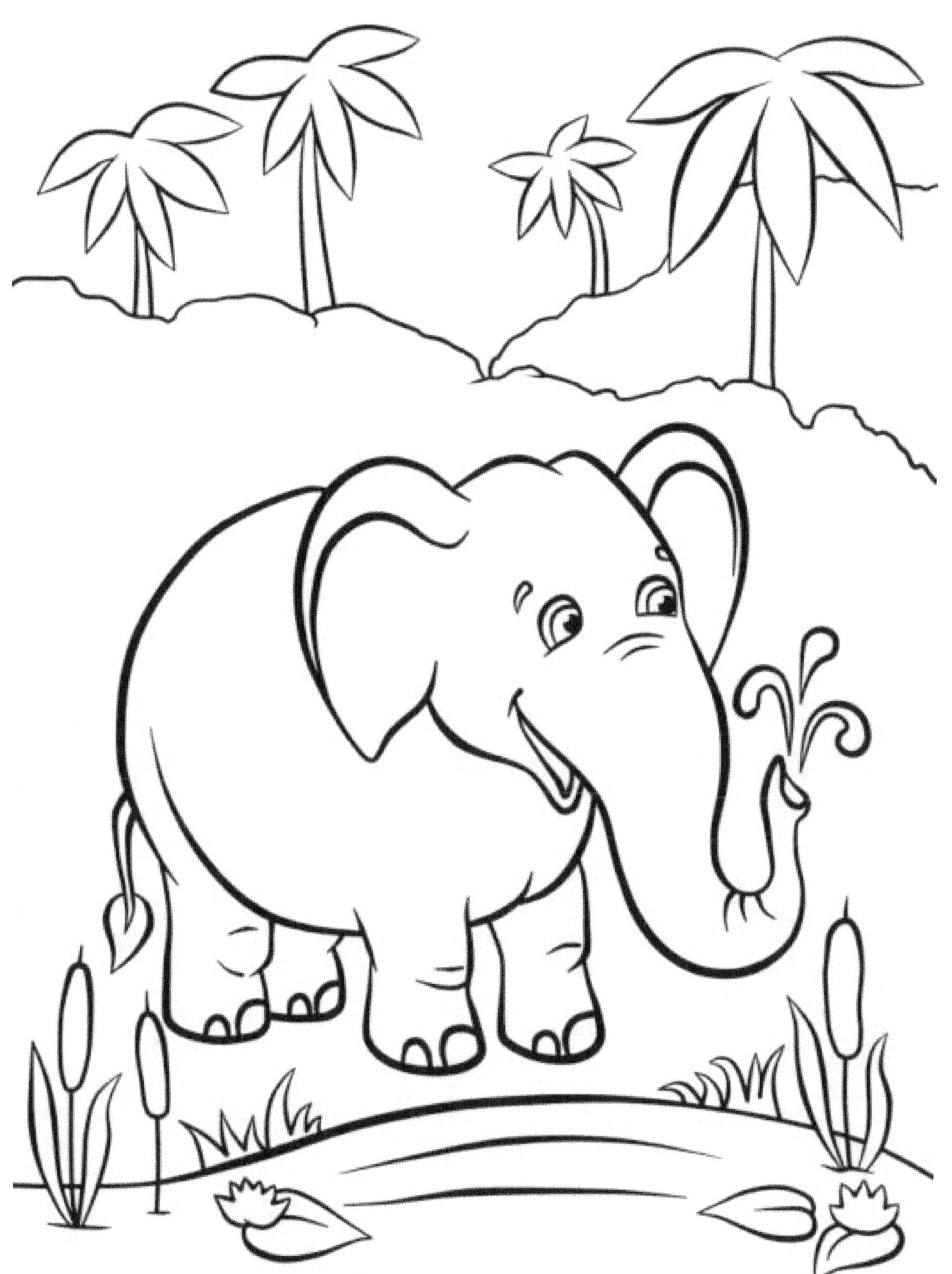

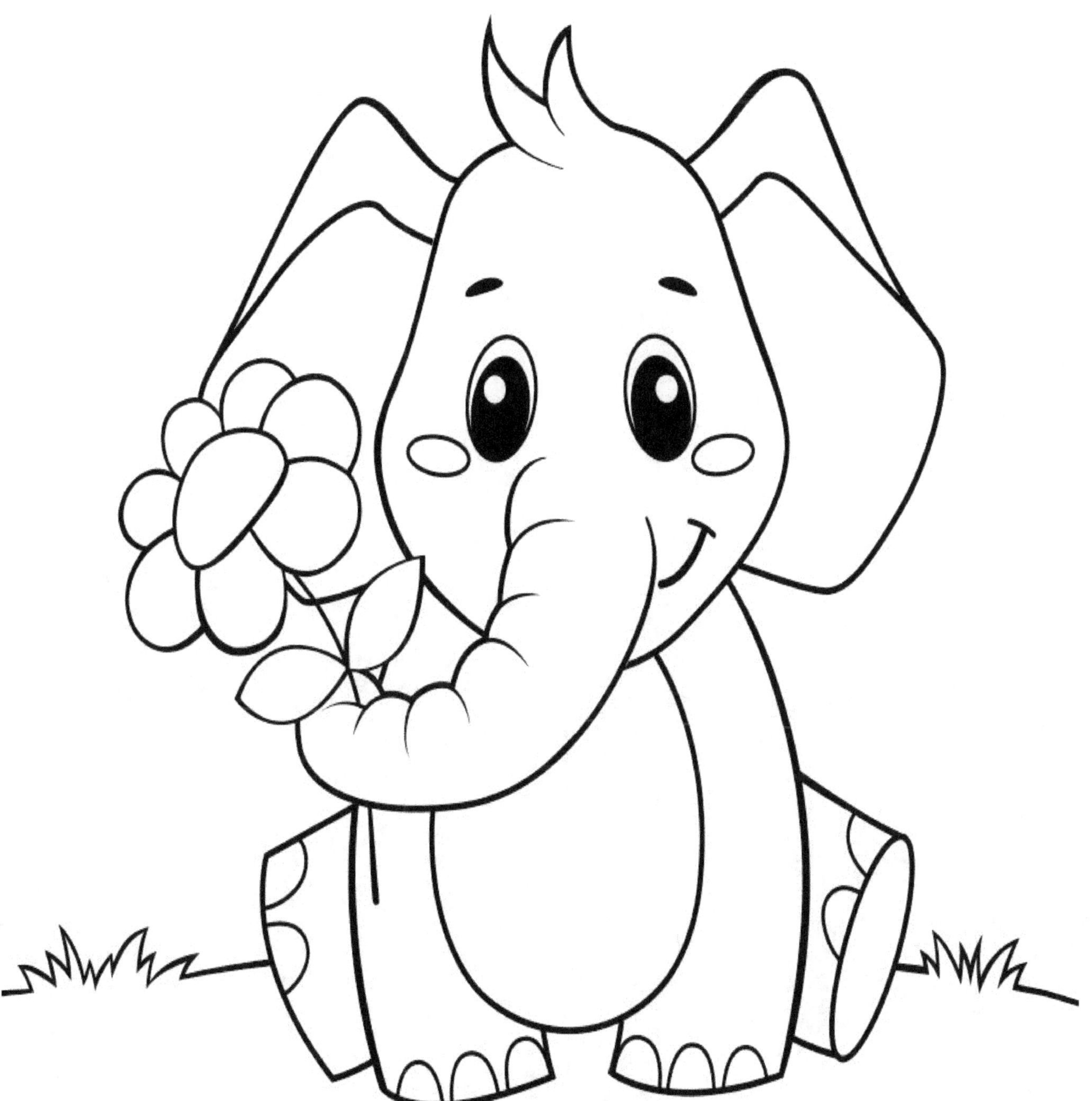

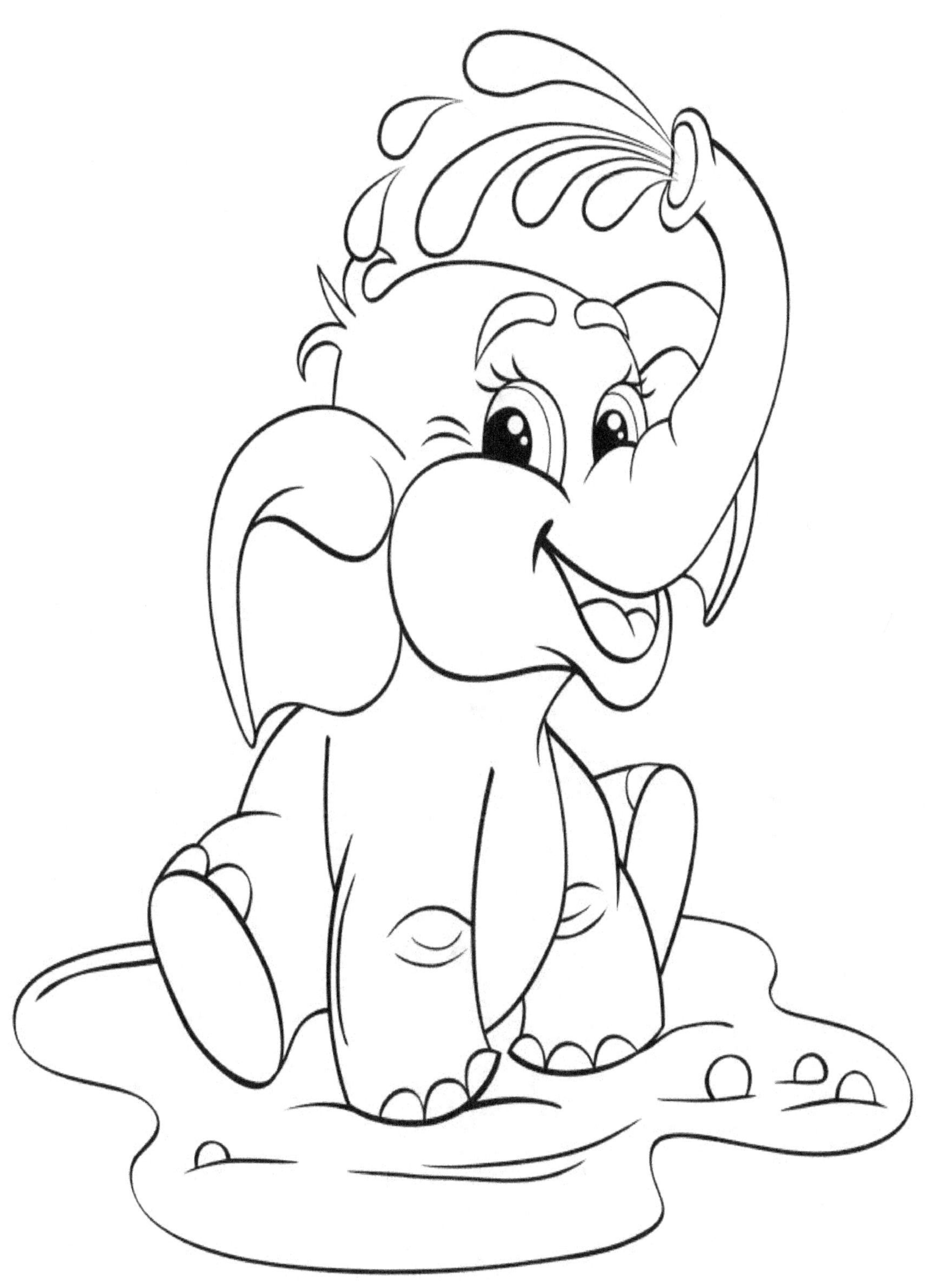

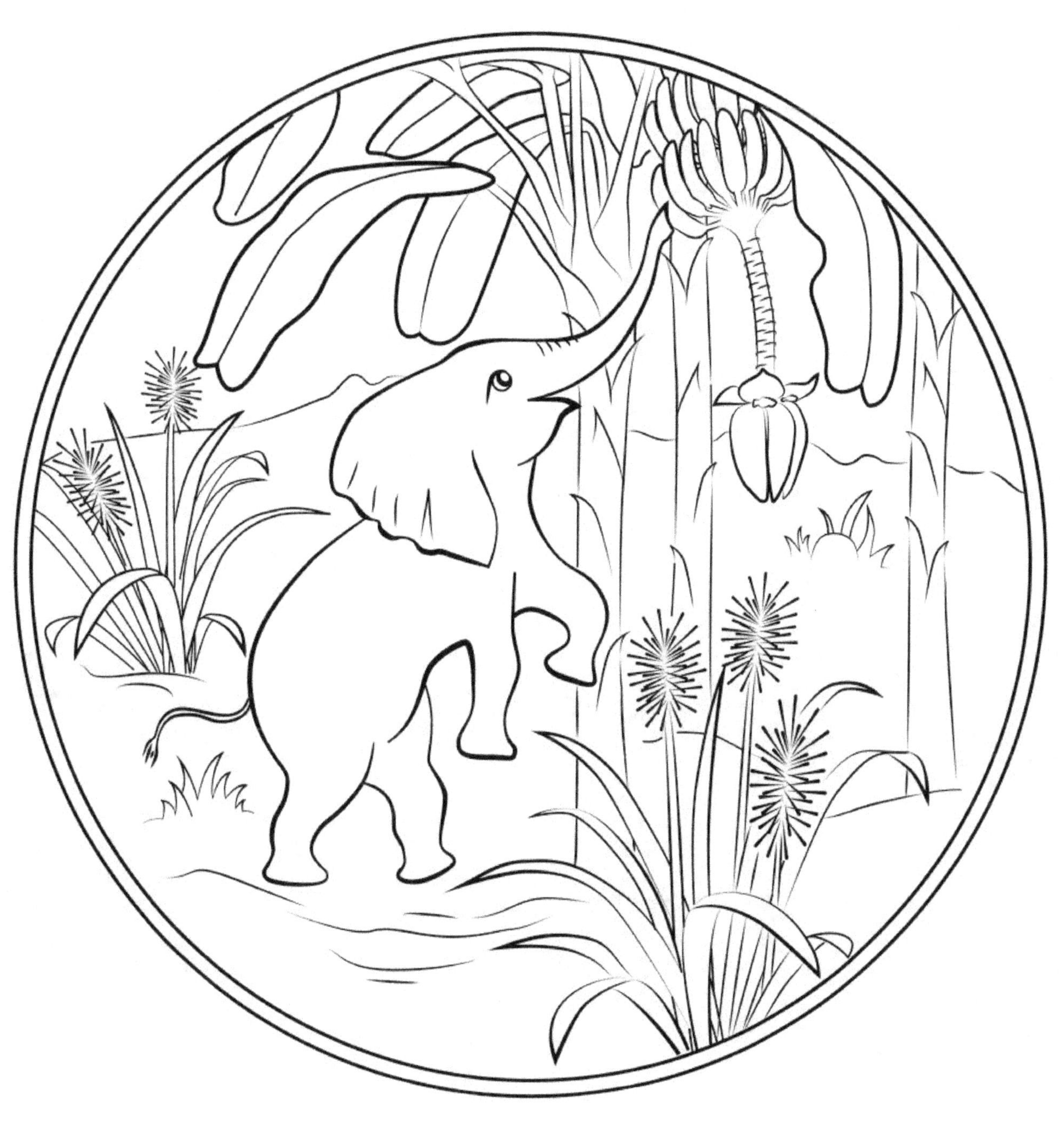

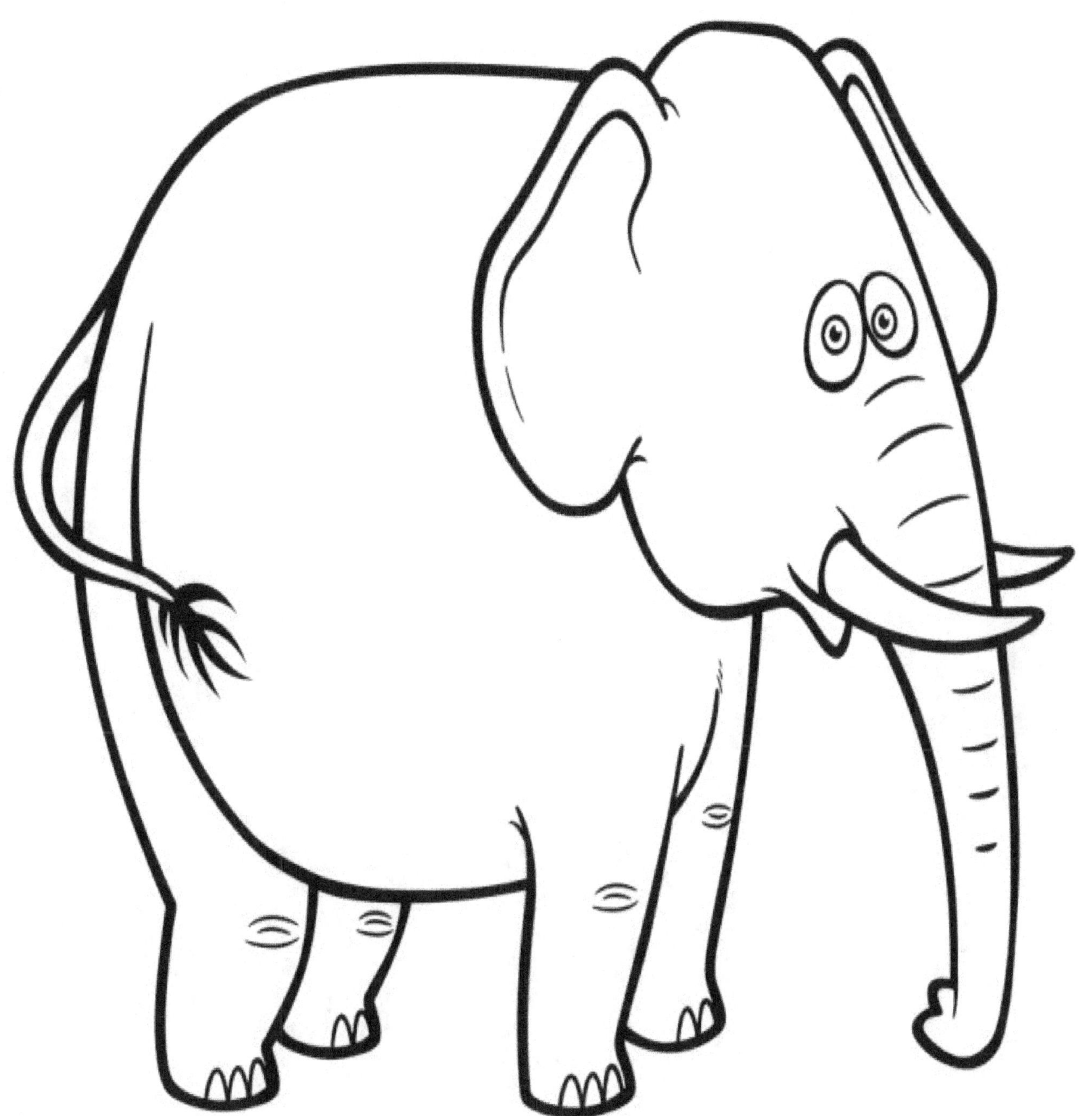

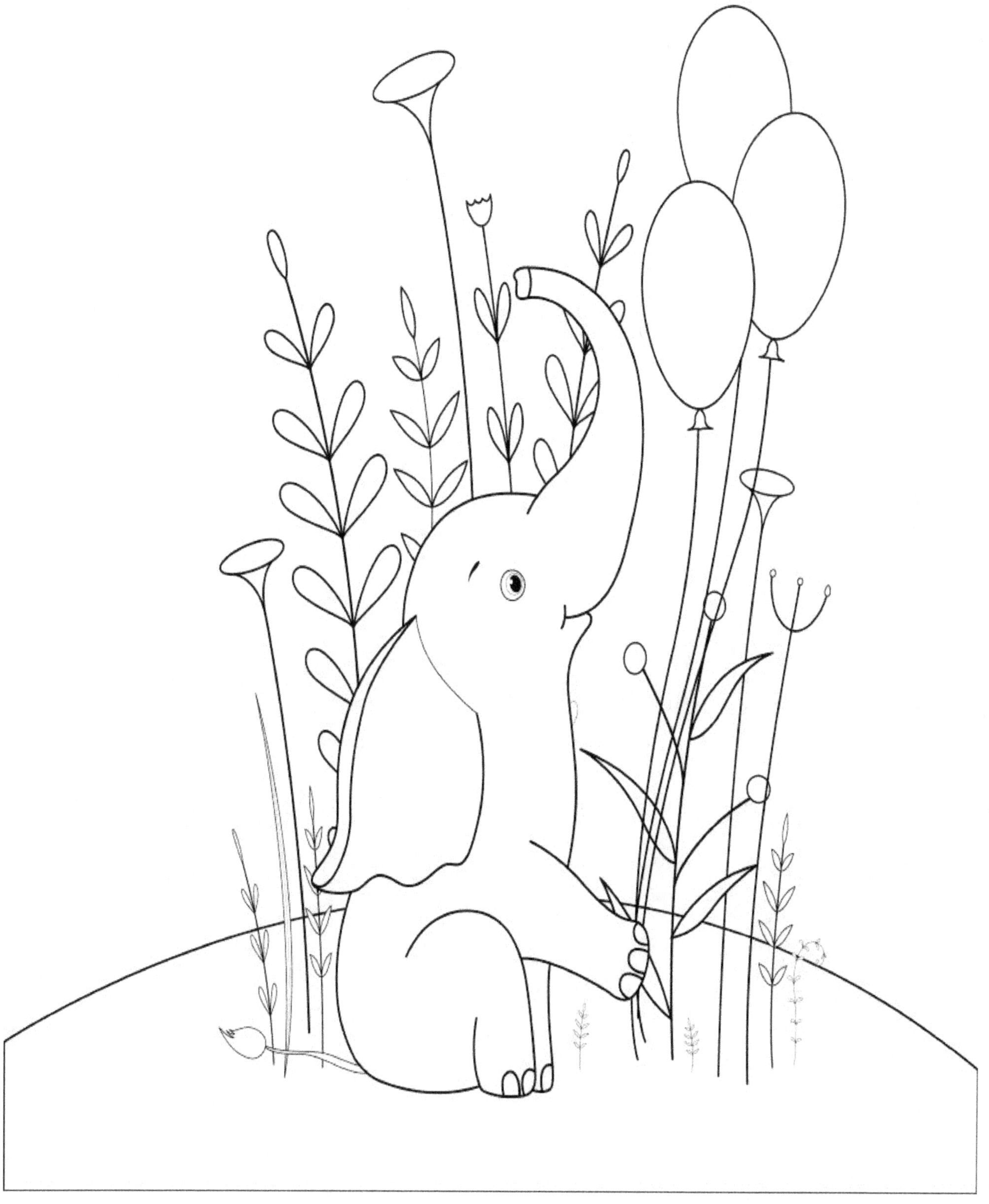

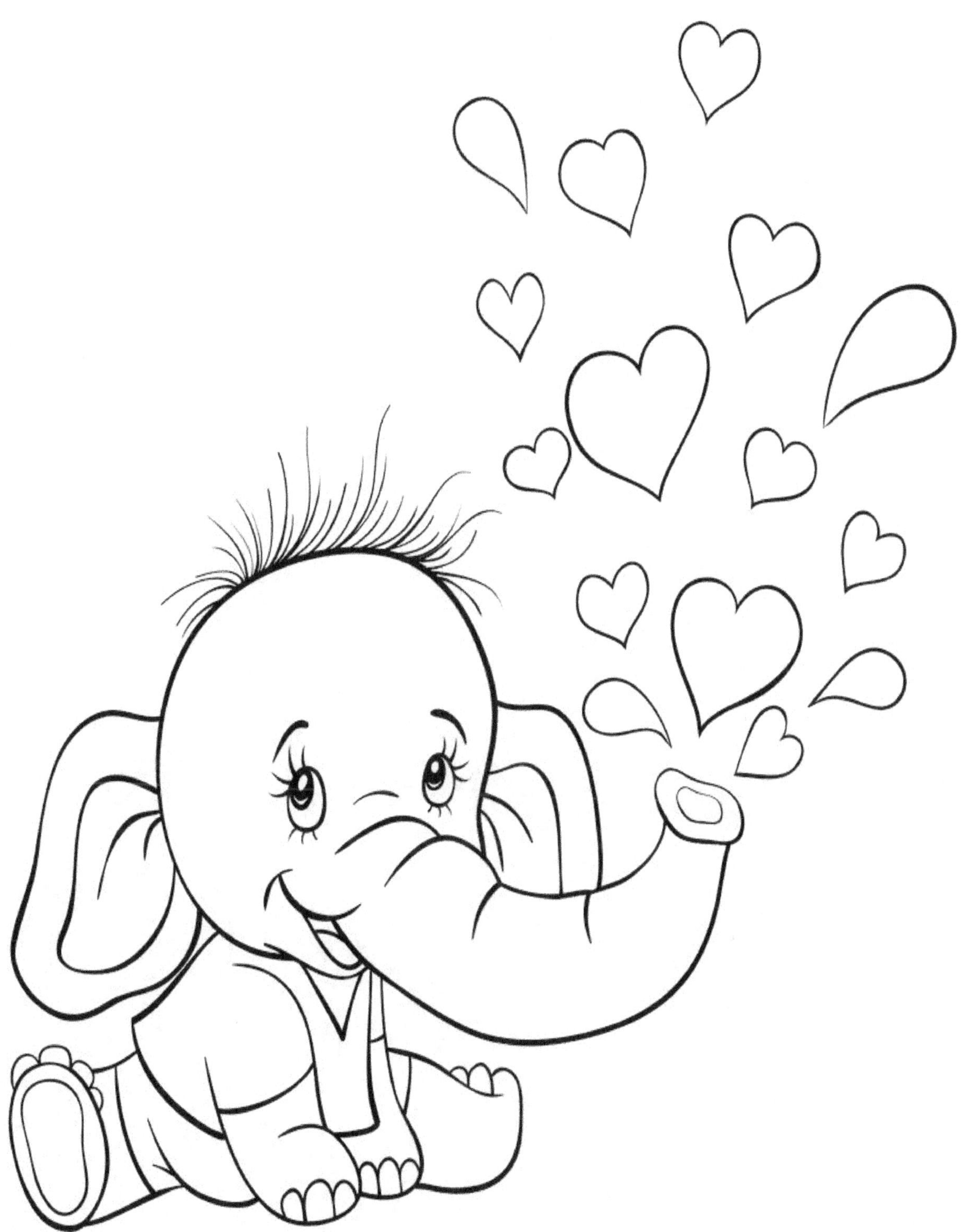

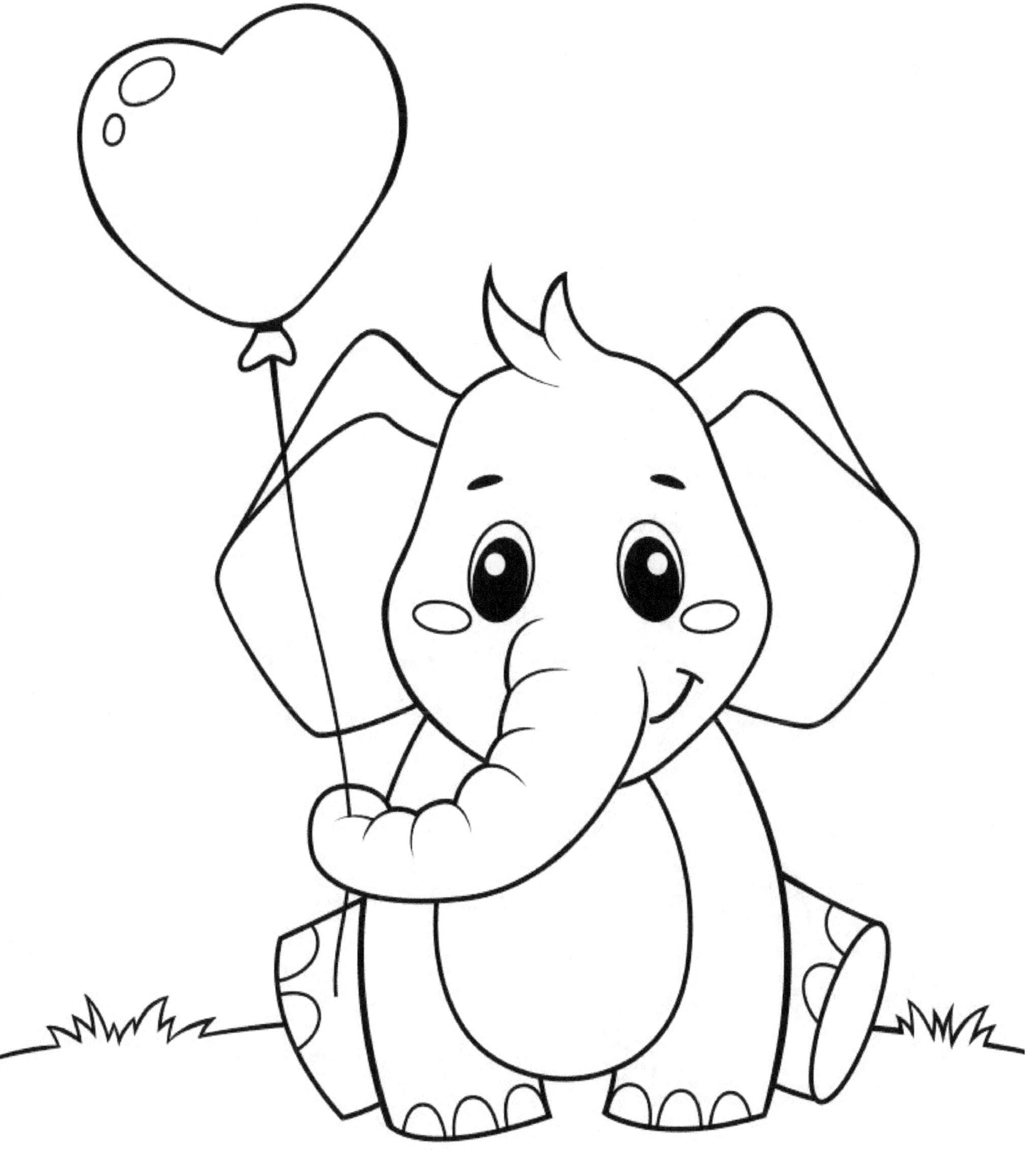

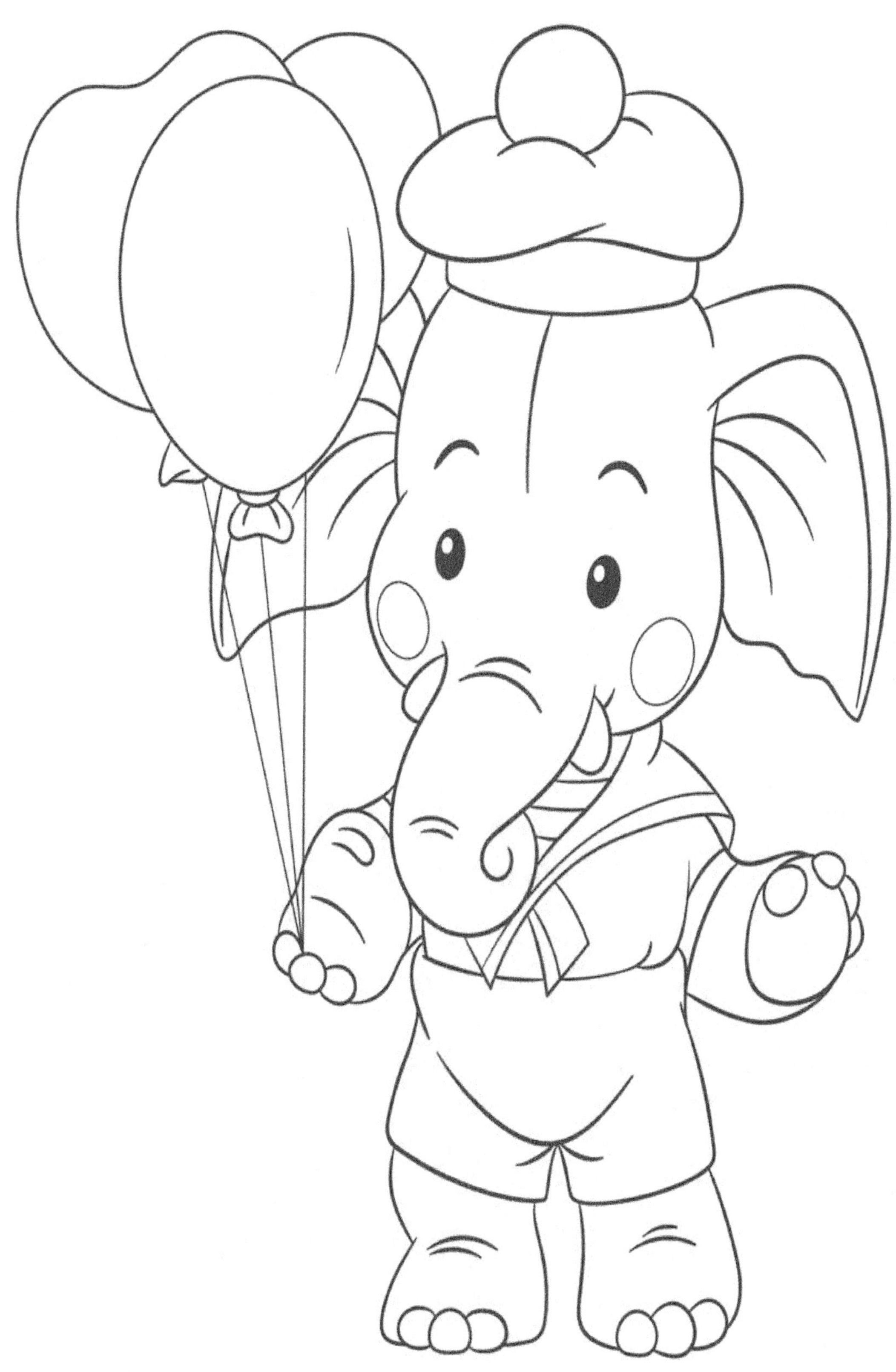

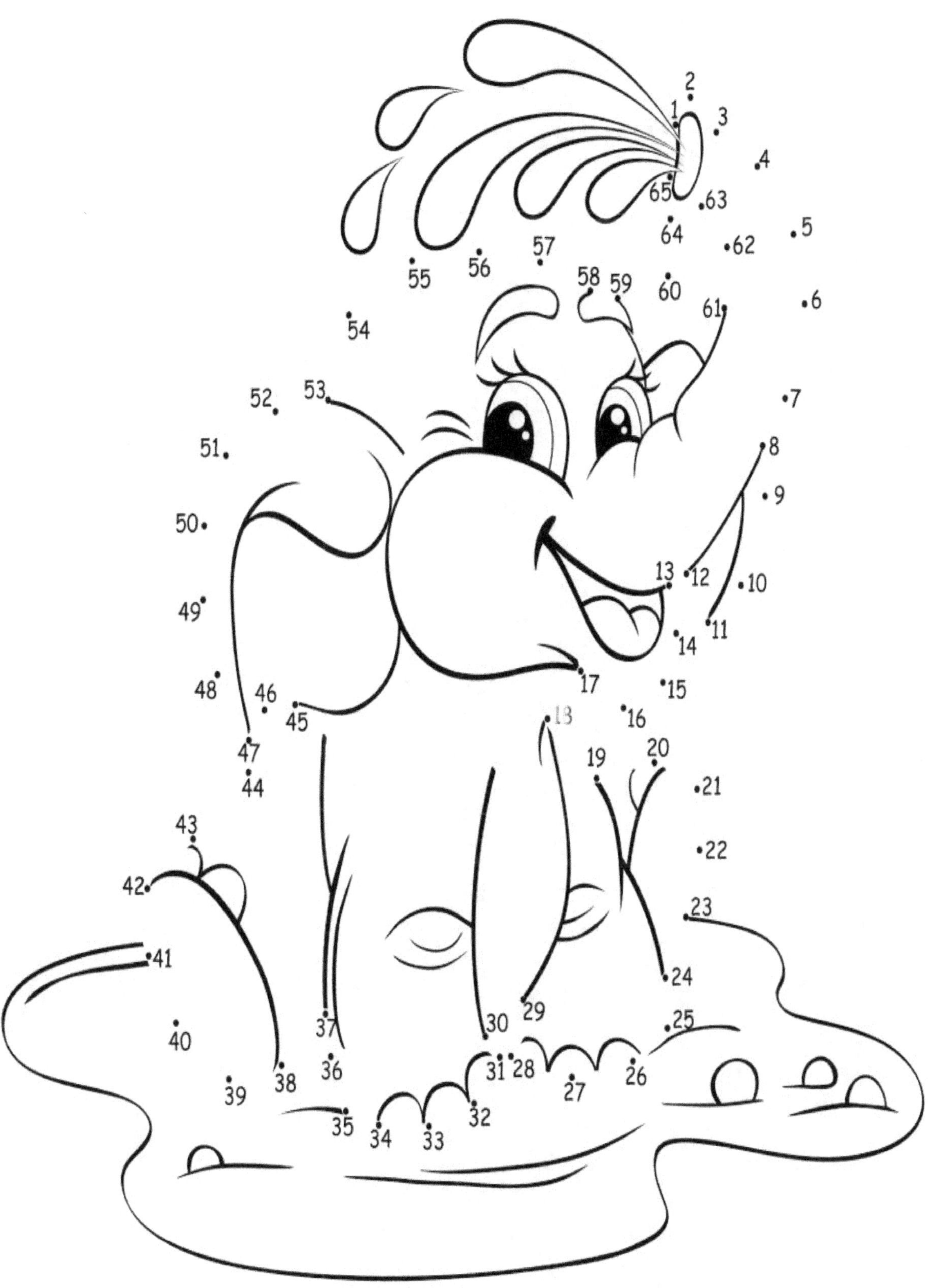

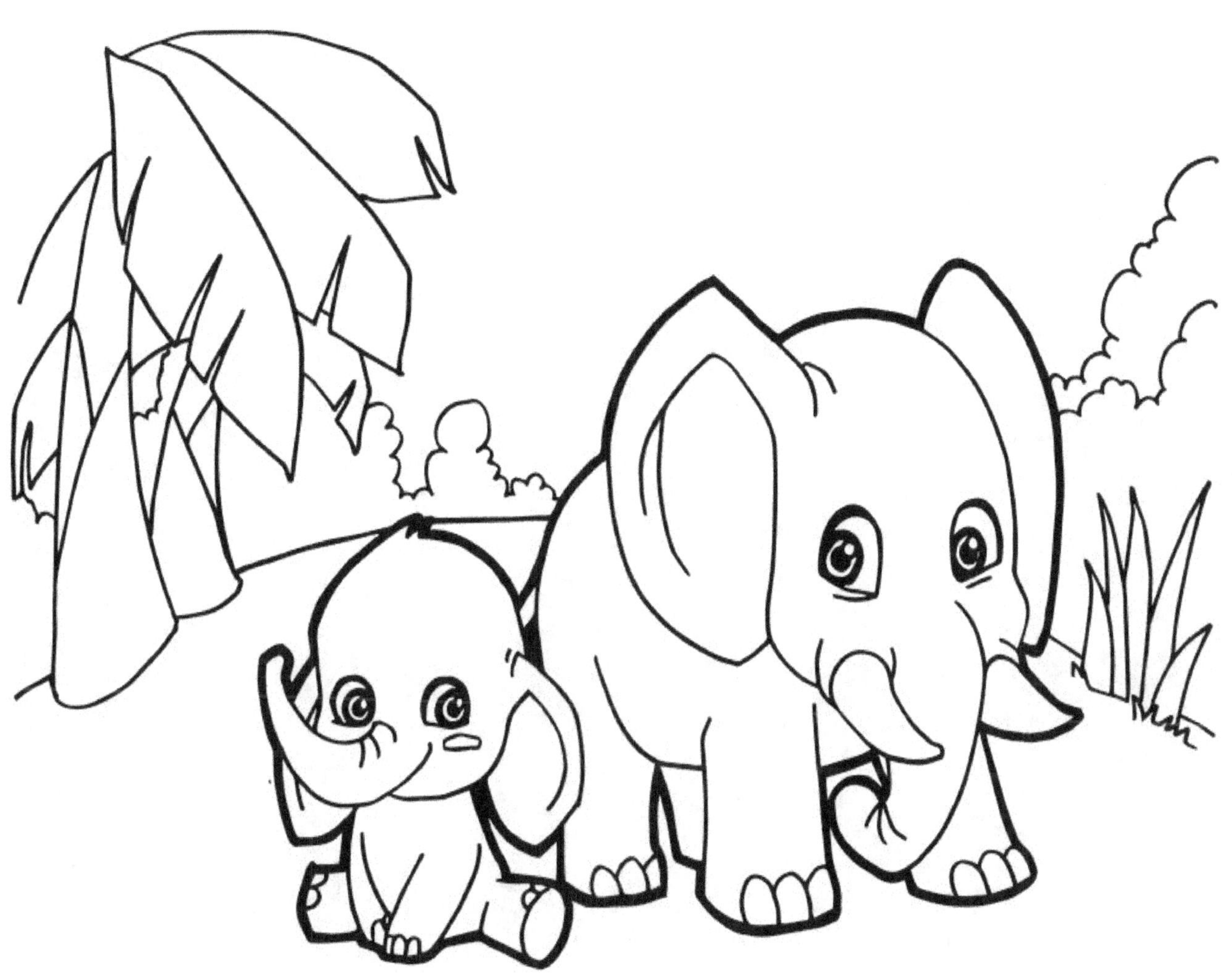

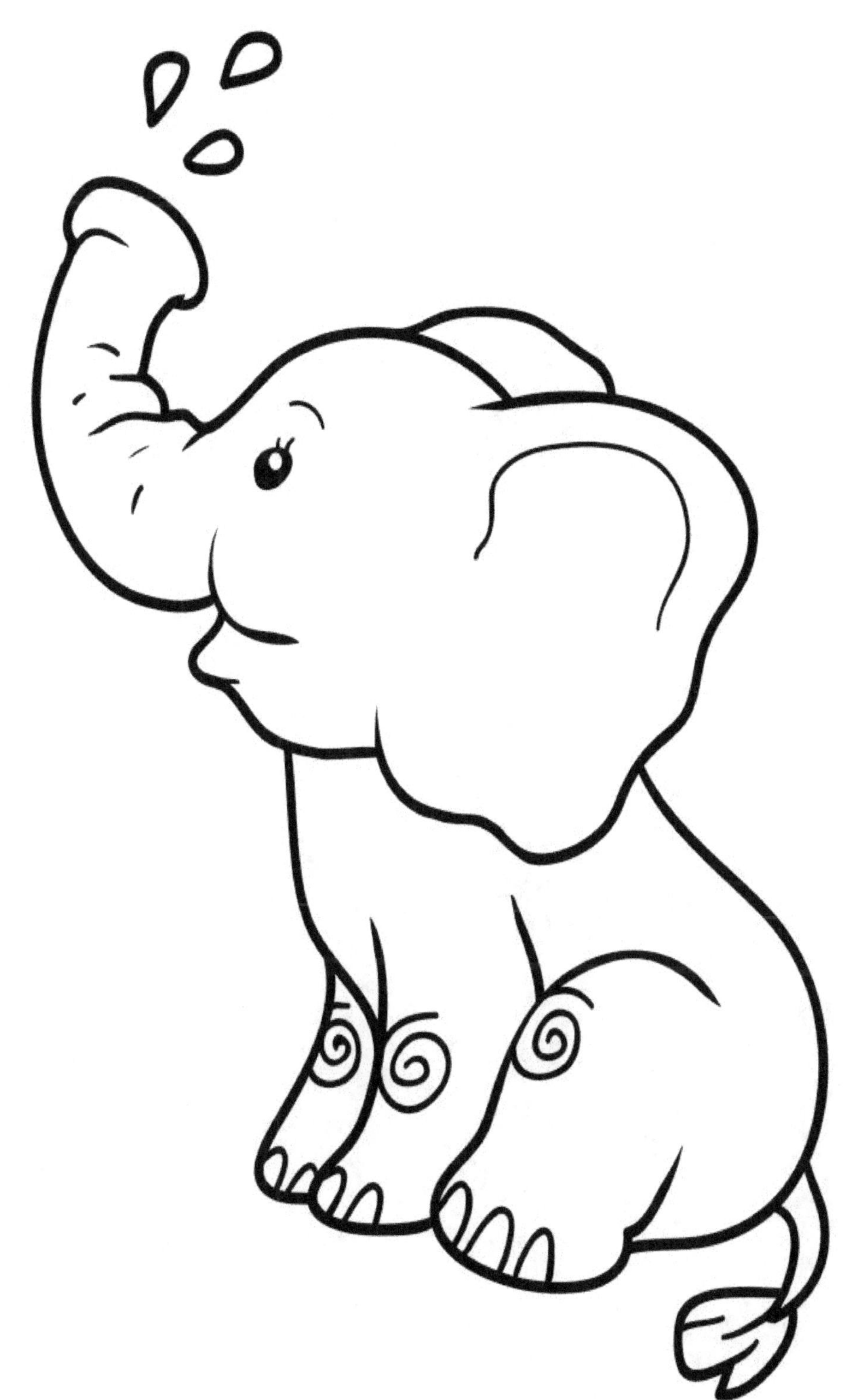

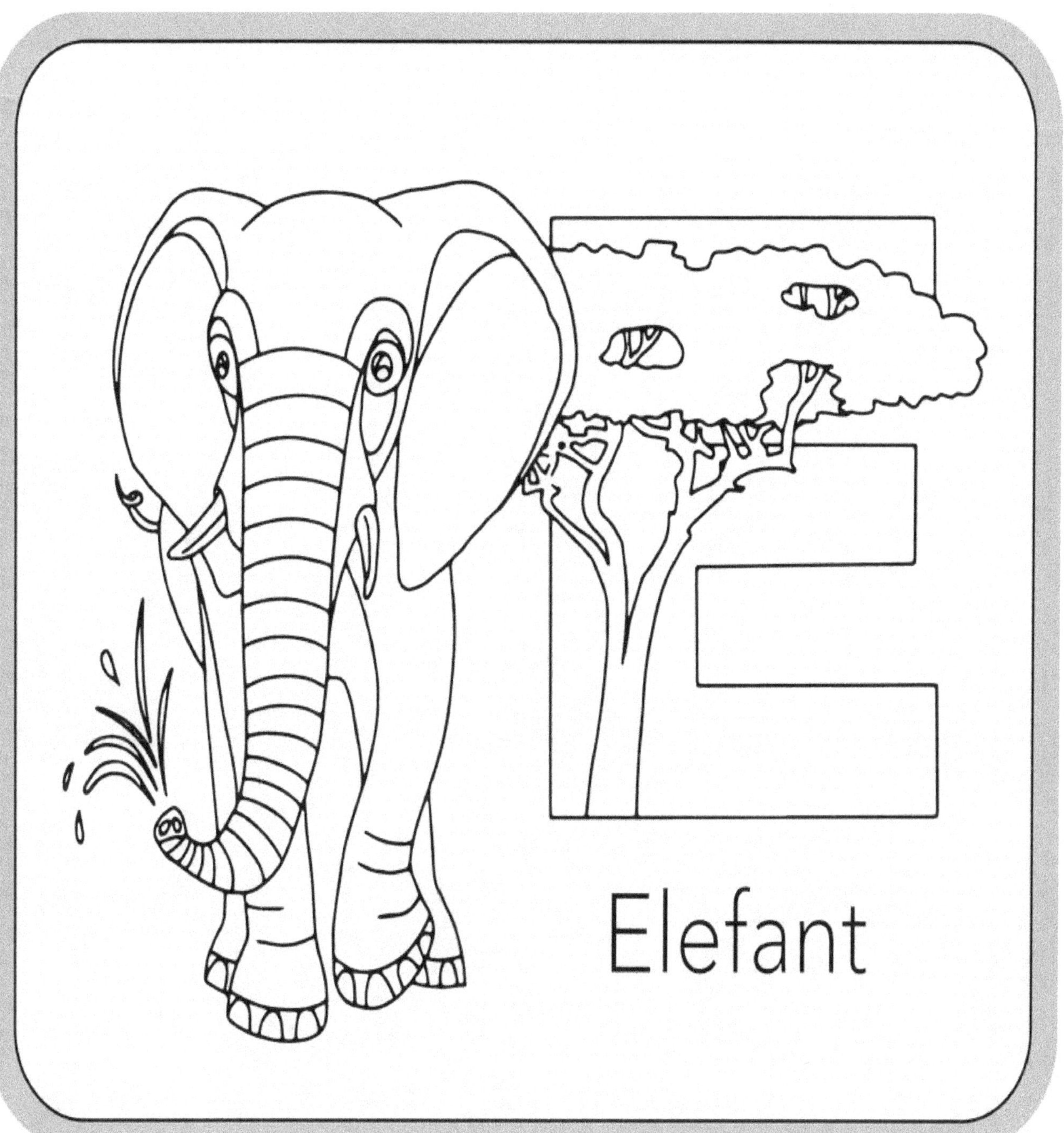

Elefant

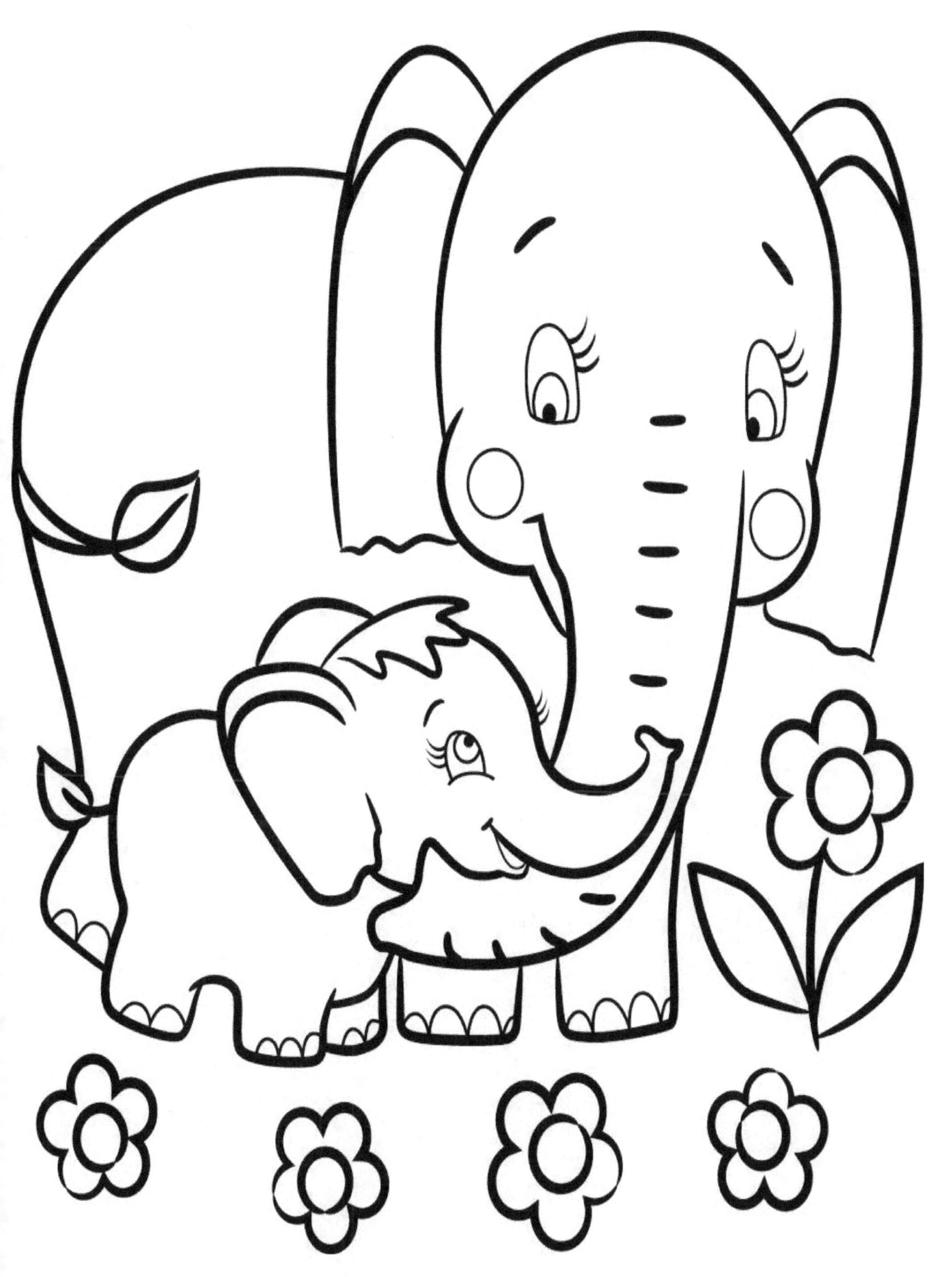

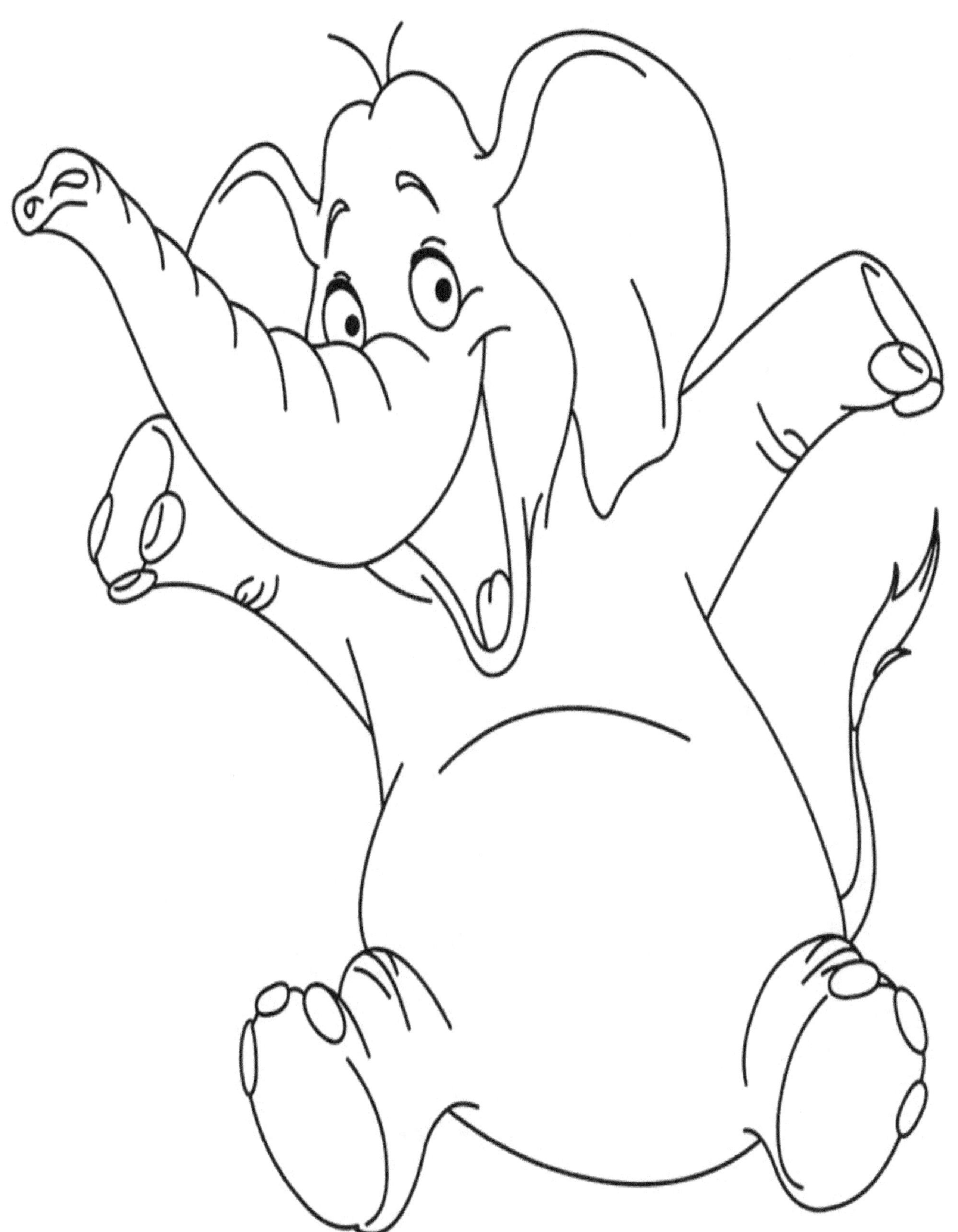

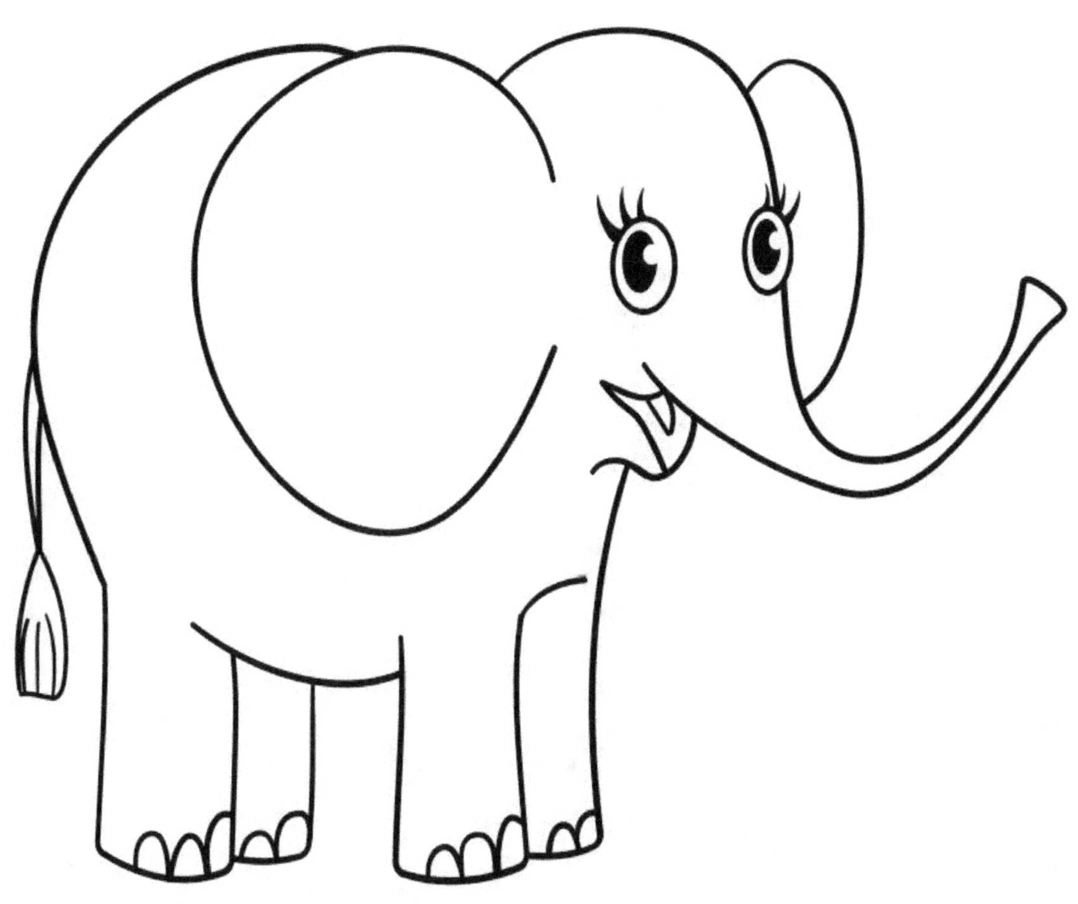

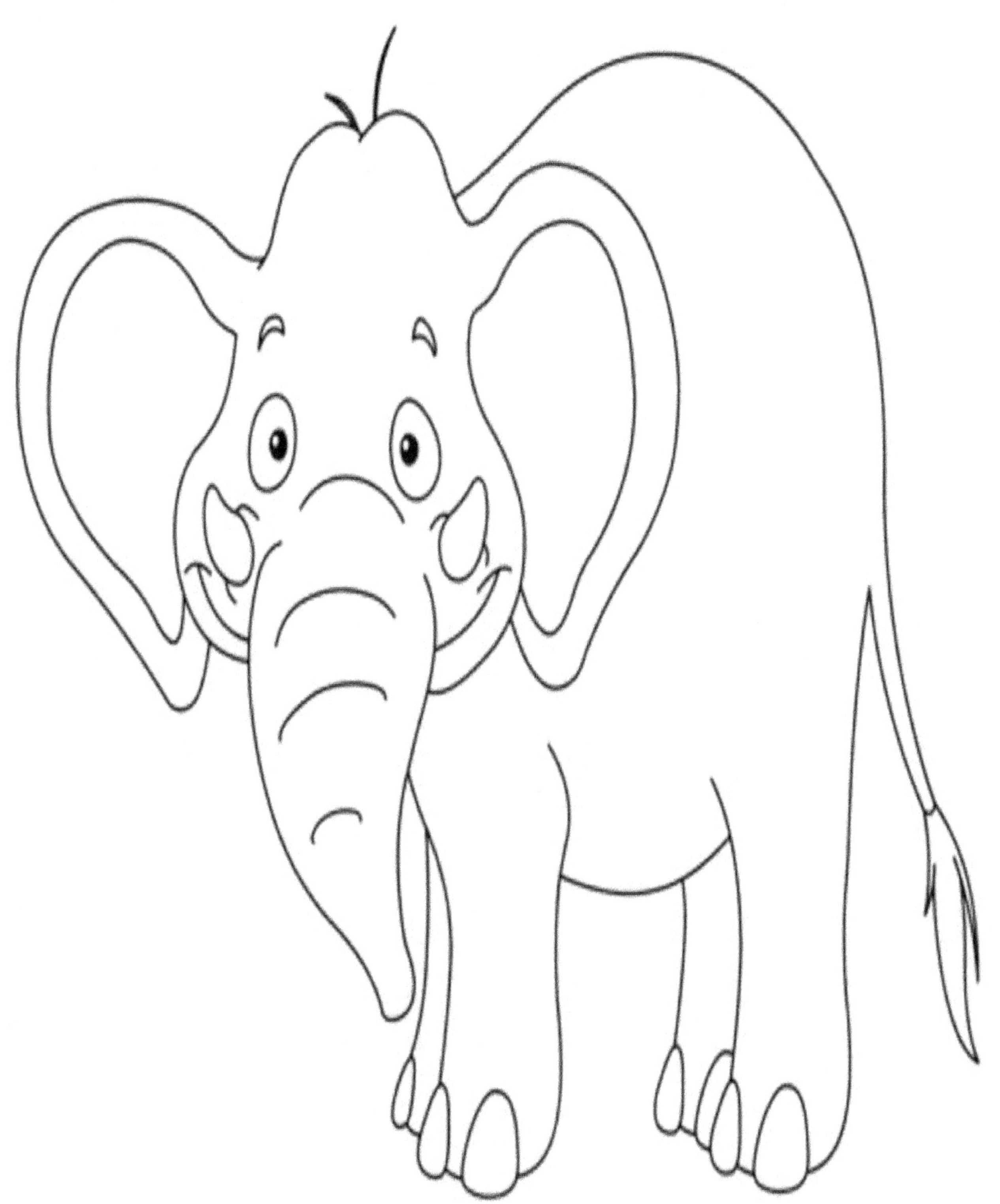

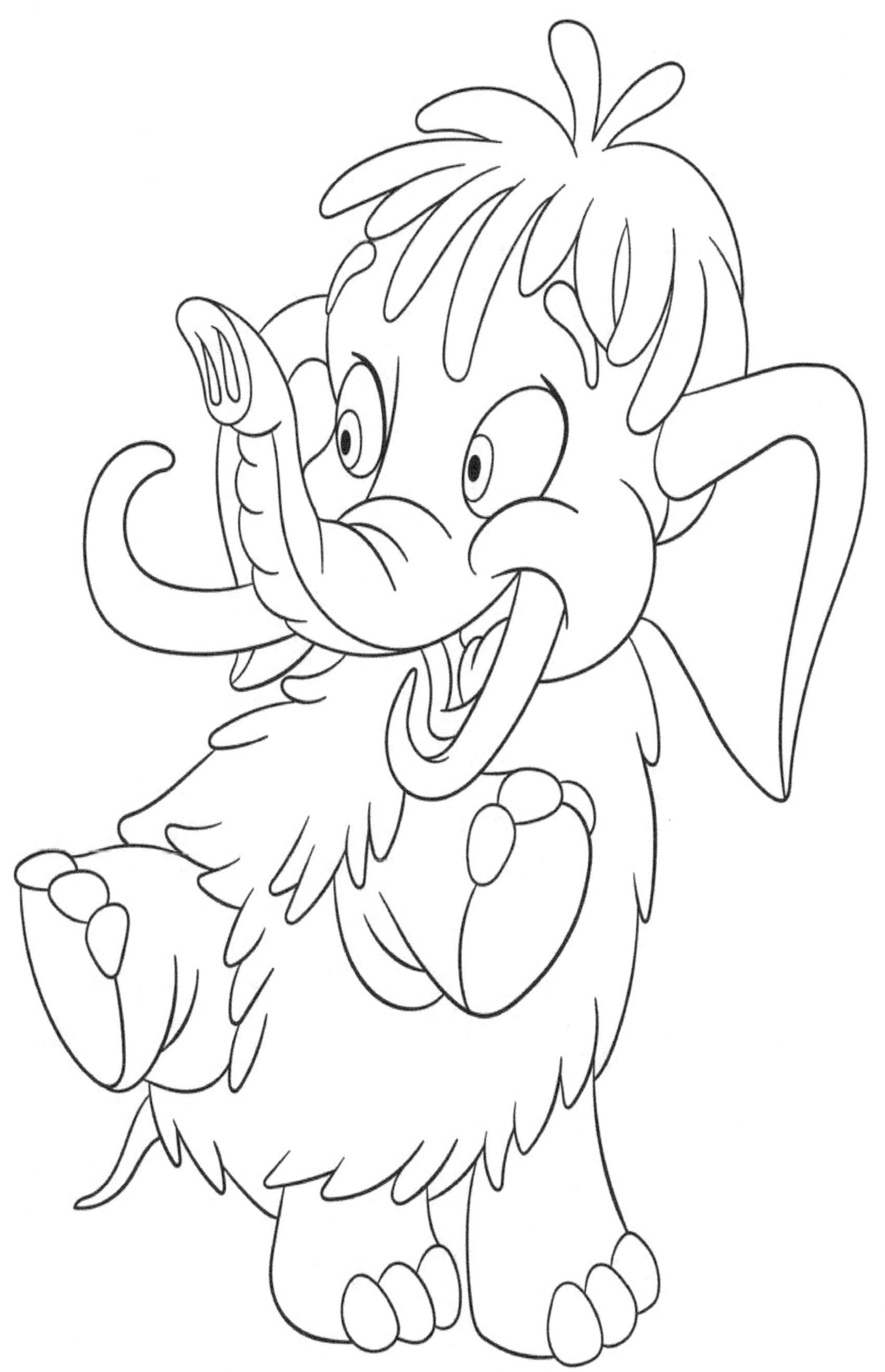

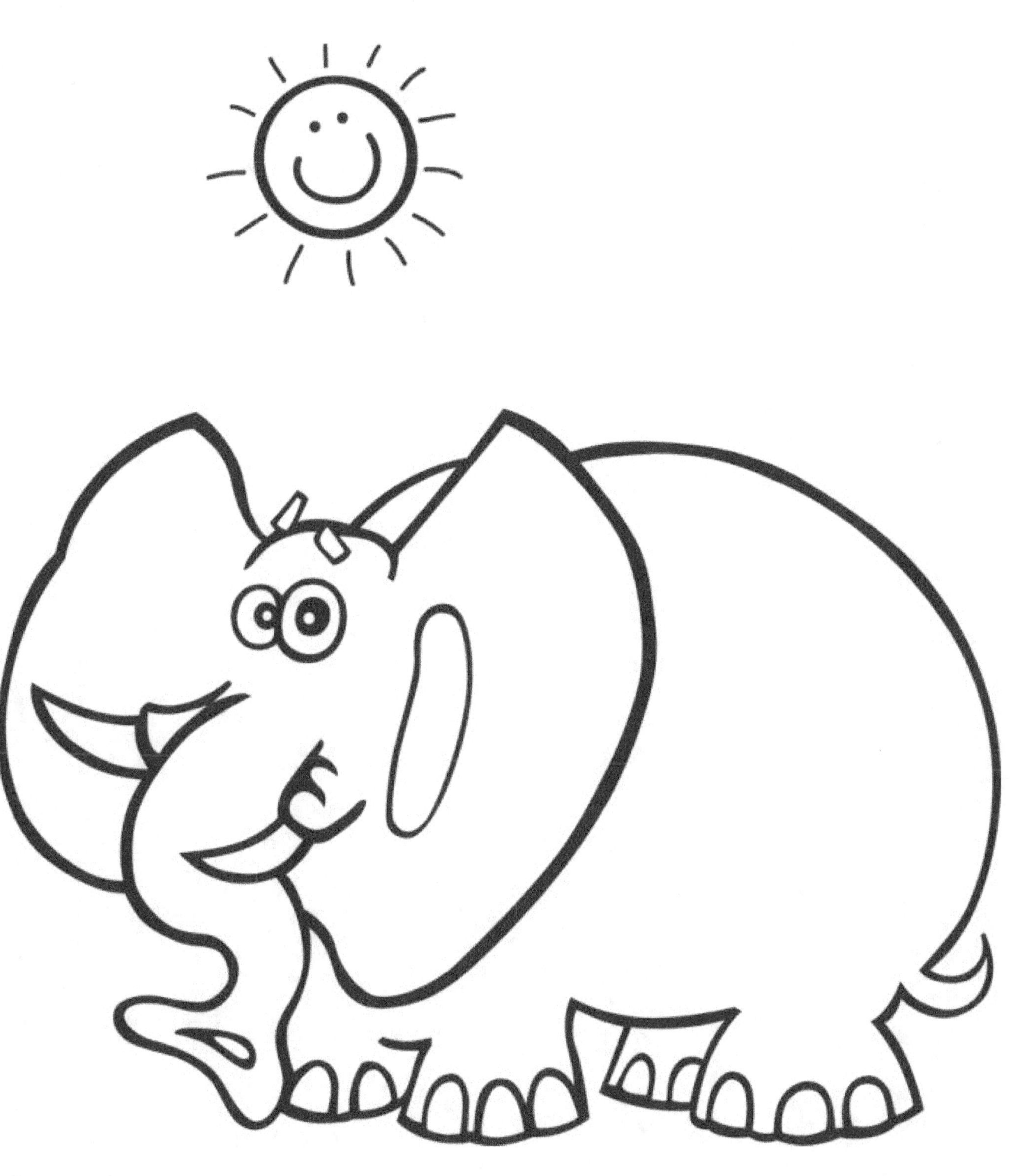

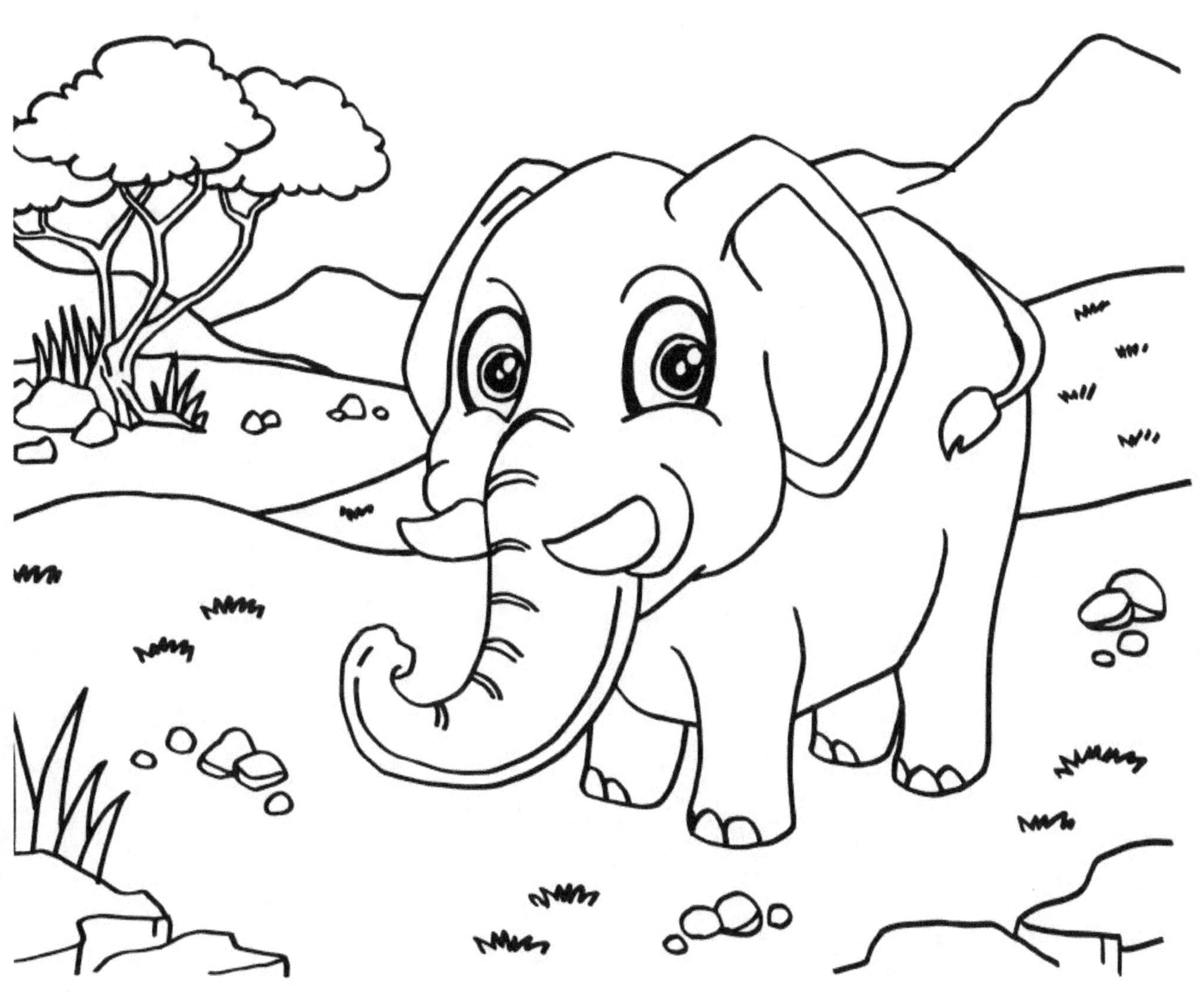

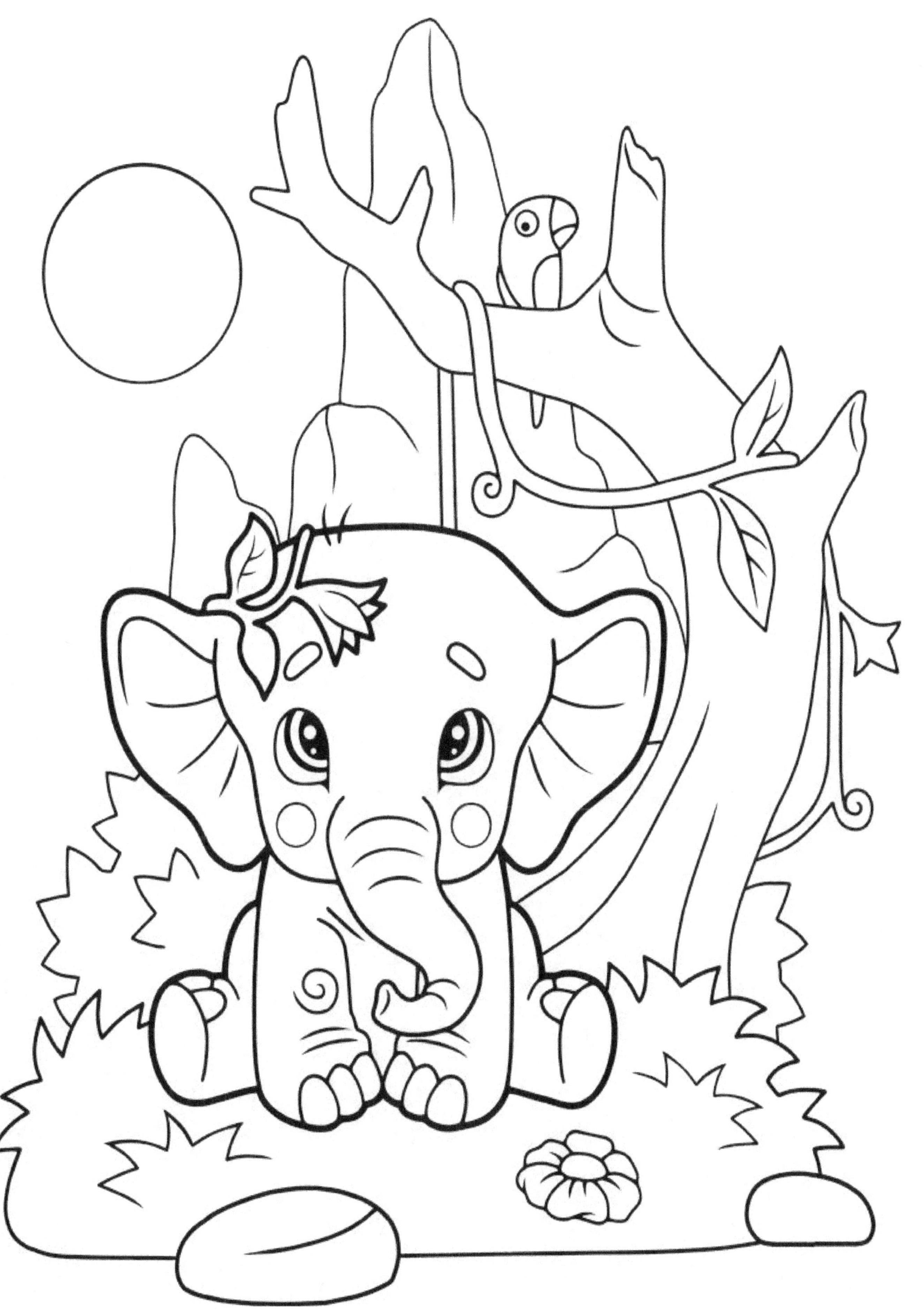

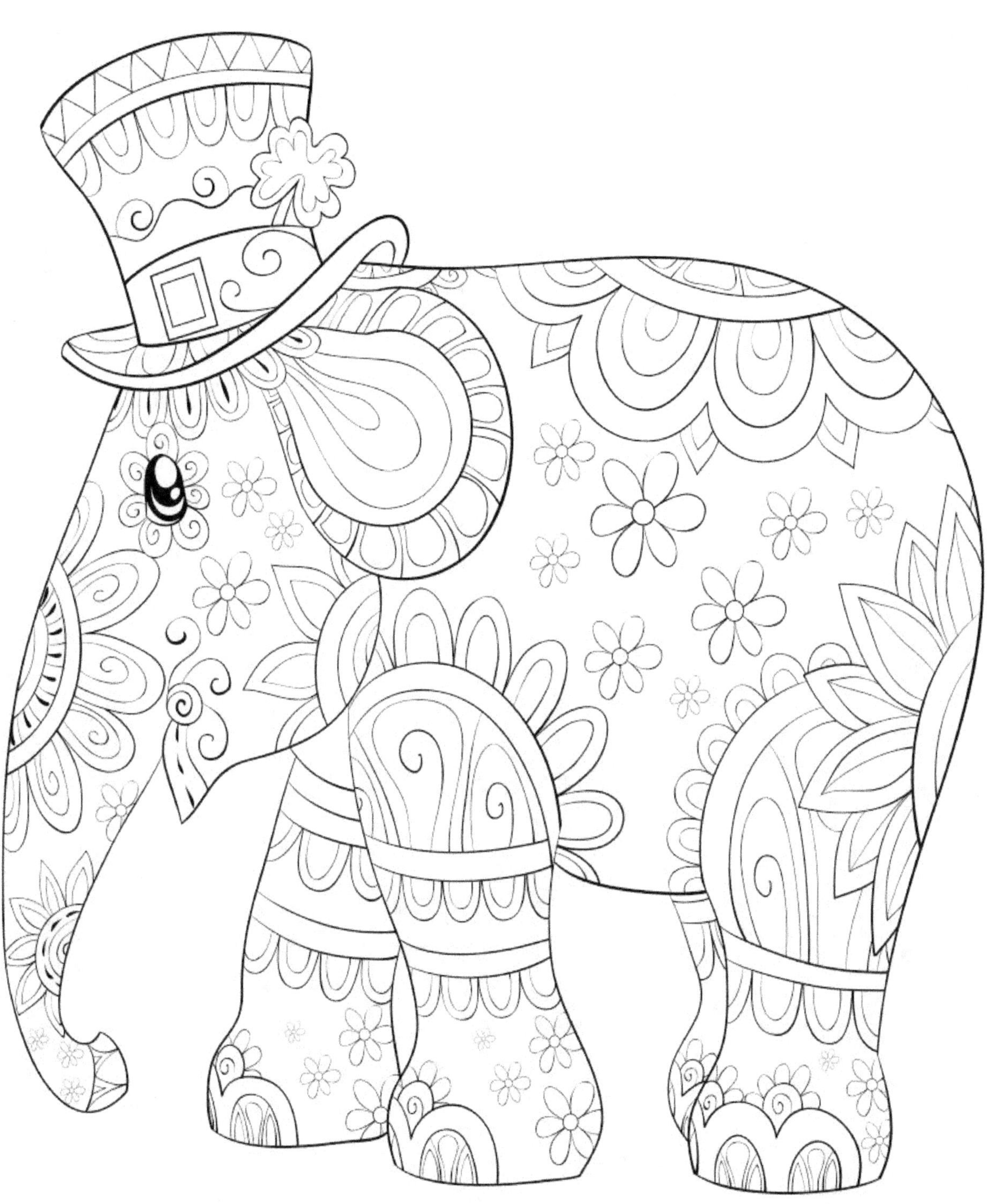

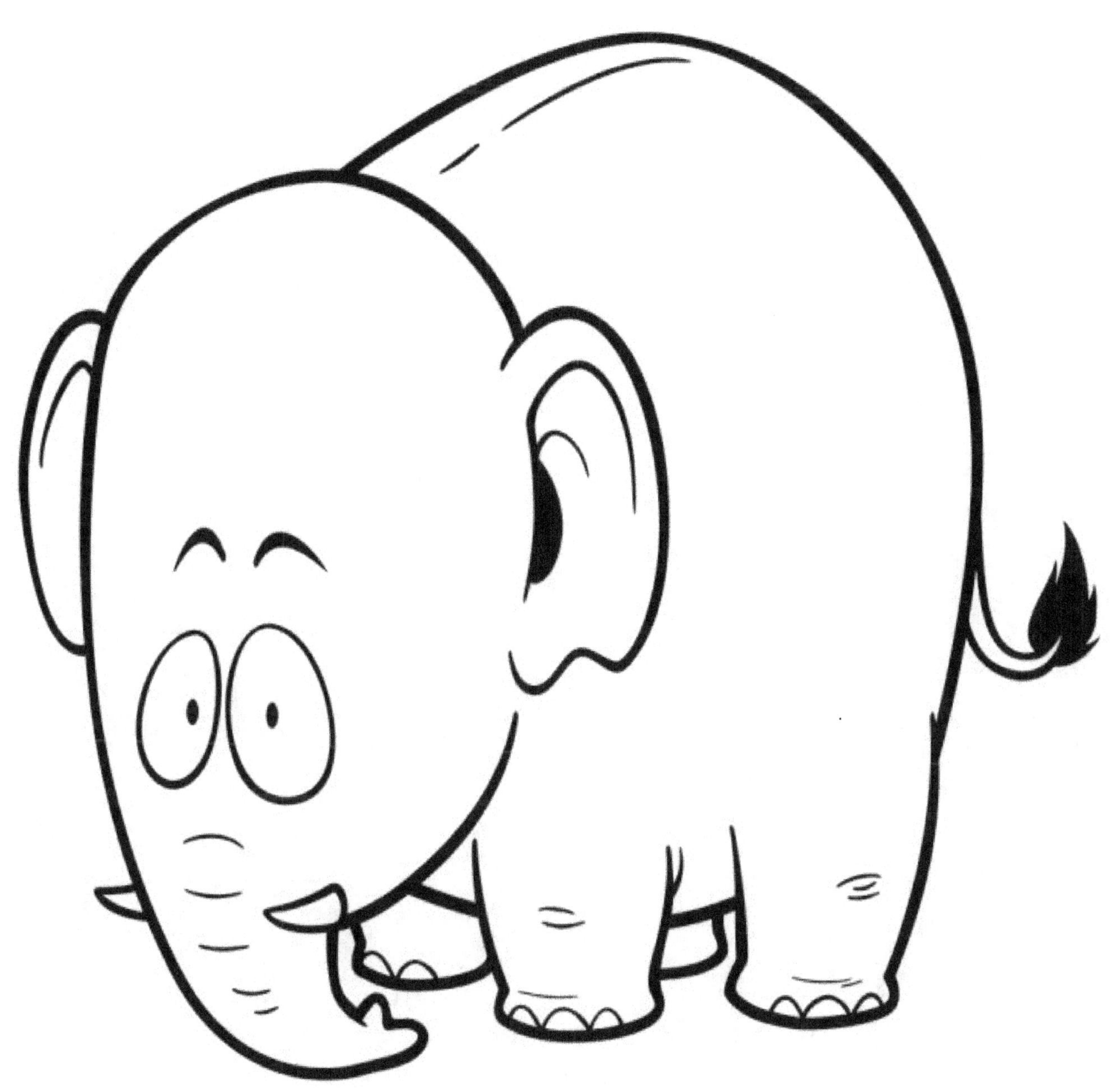

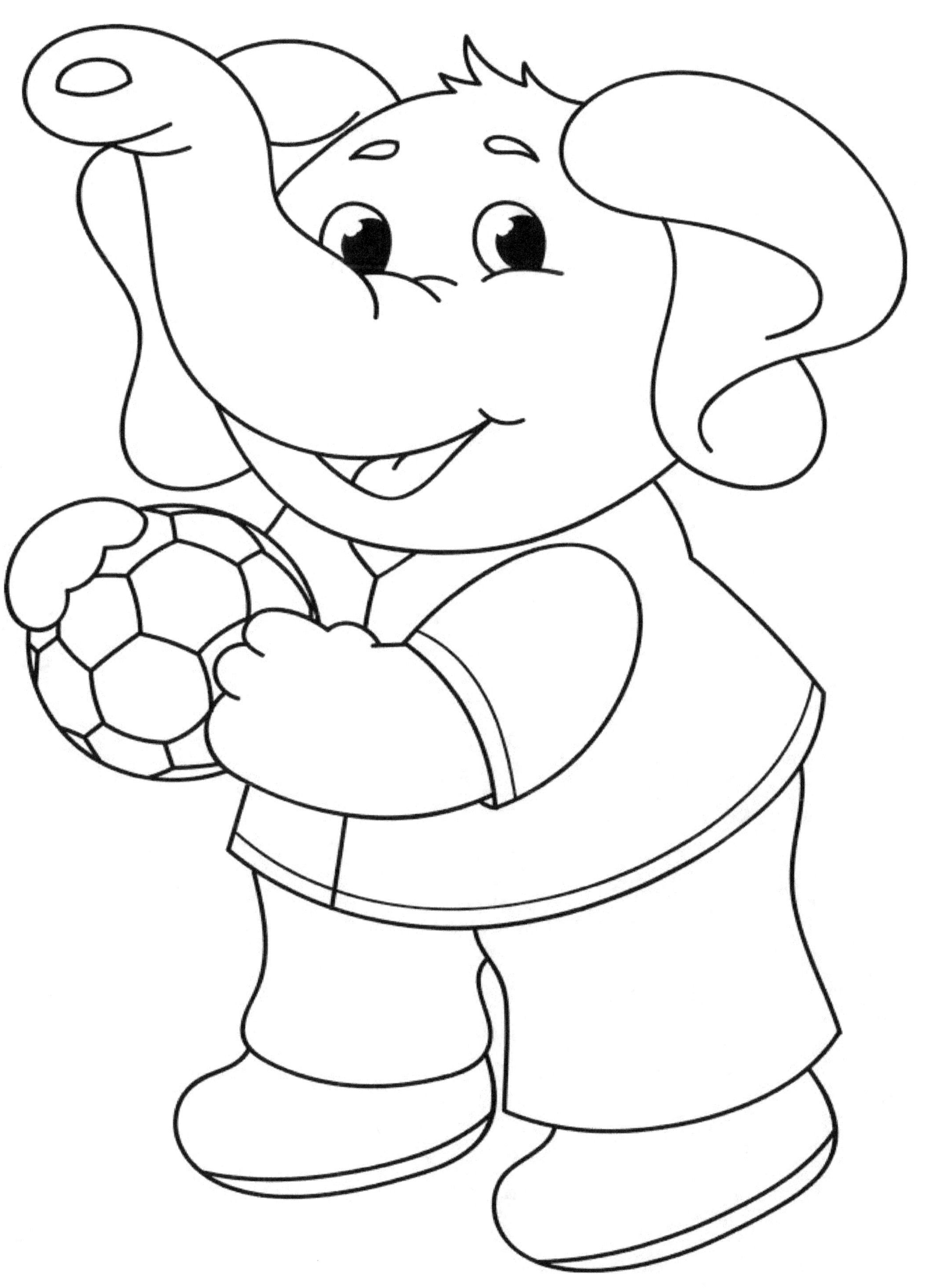

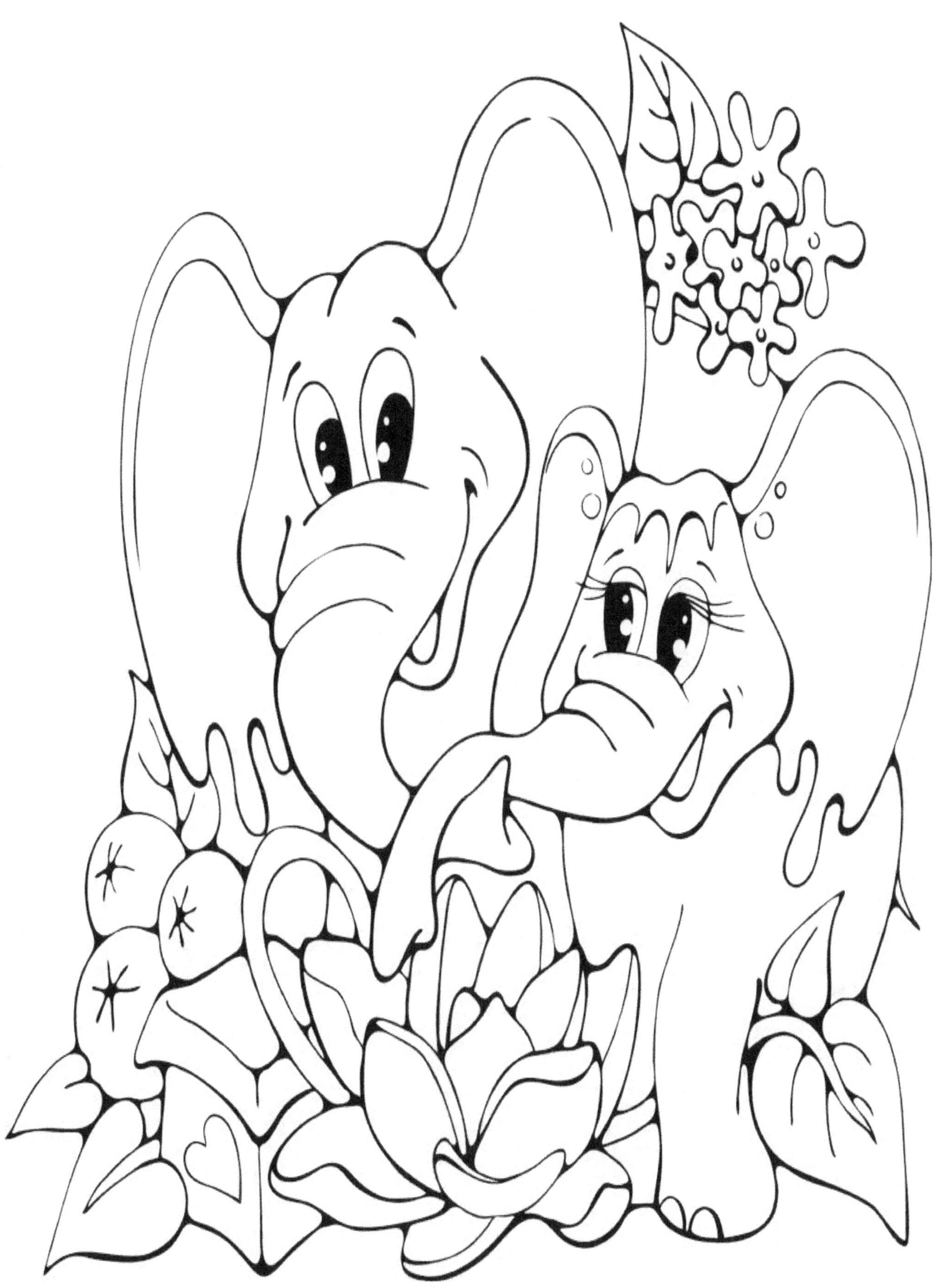

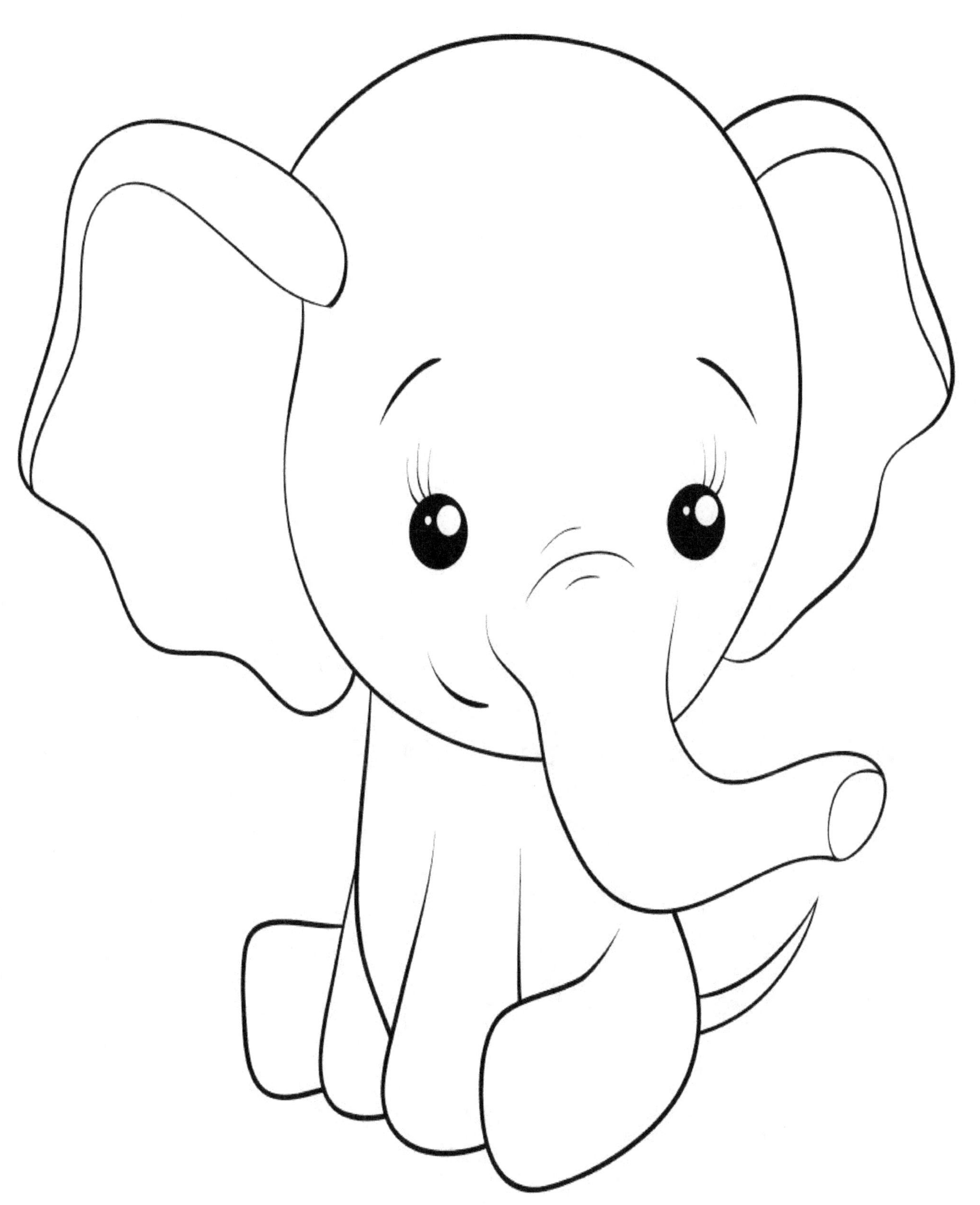

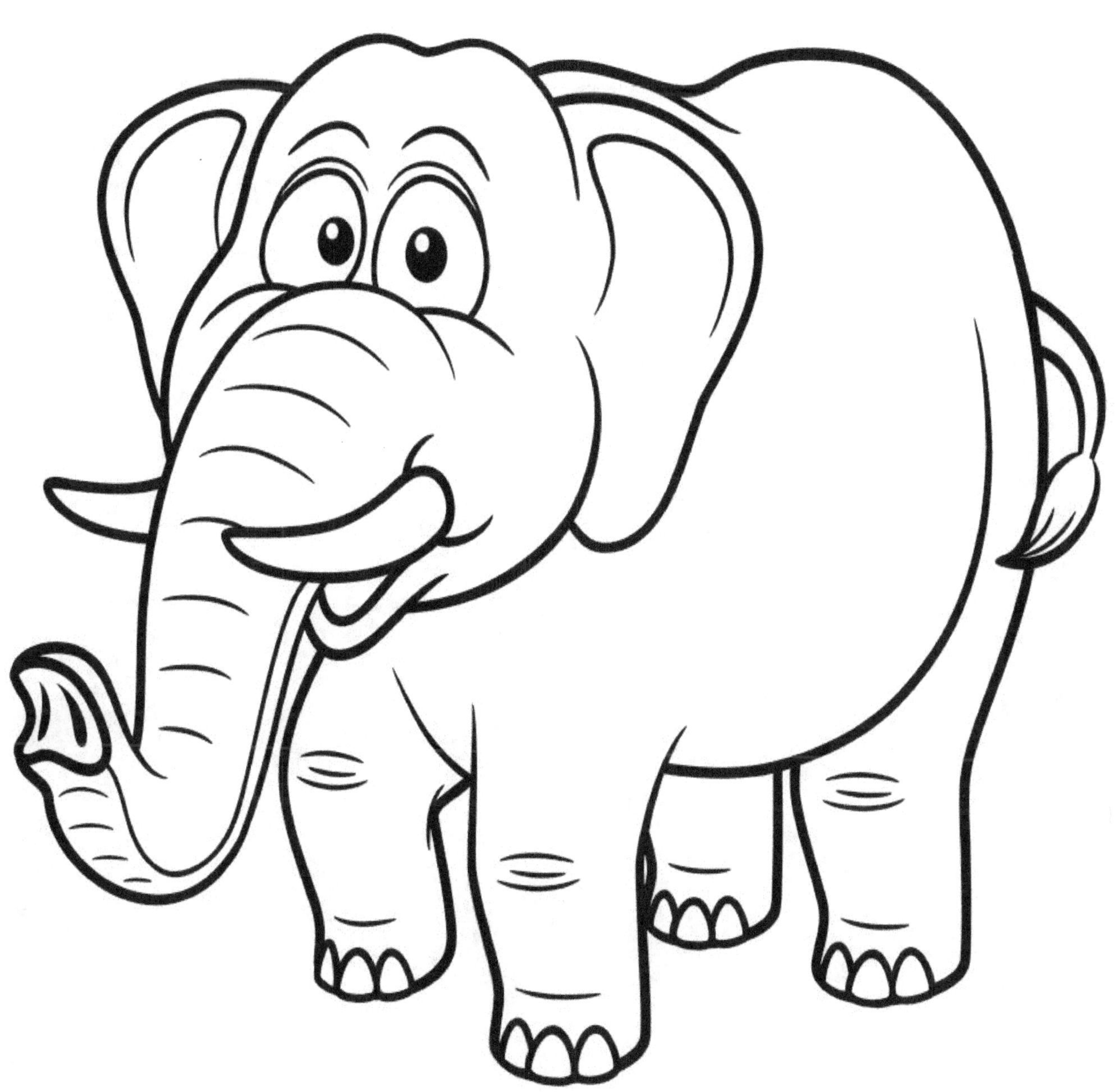

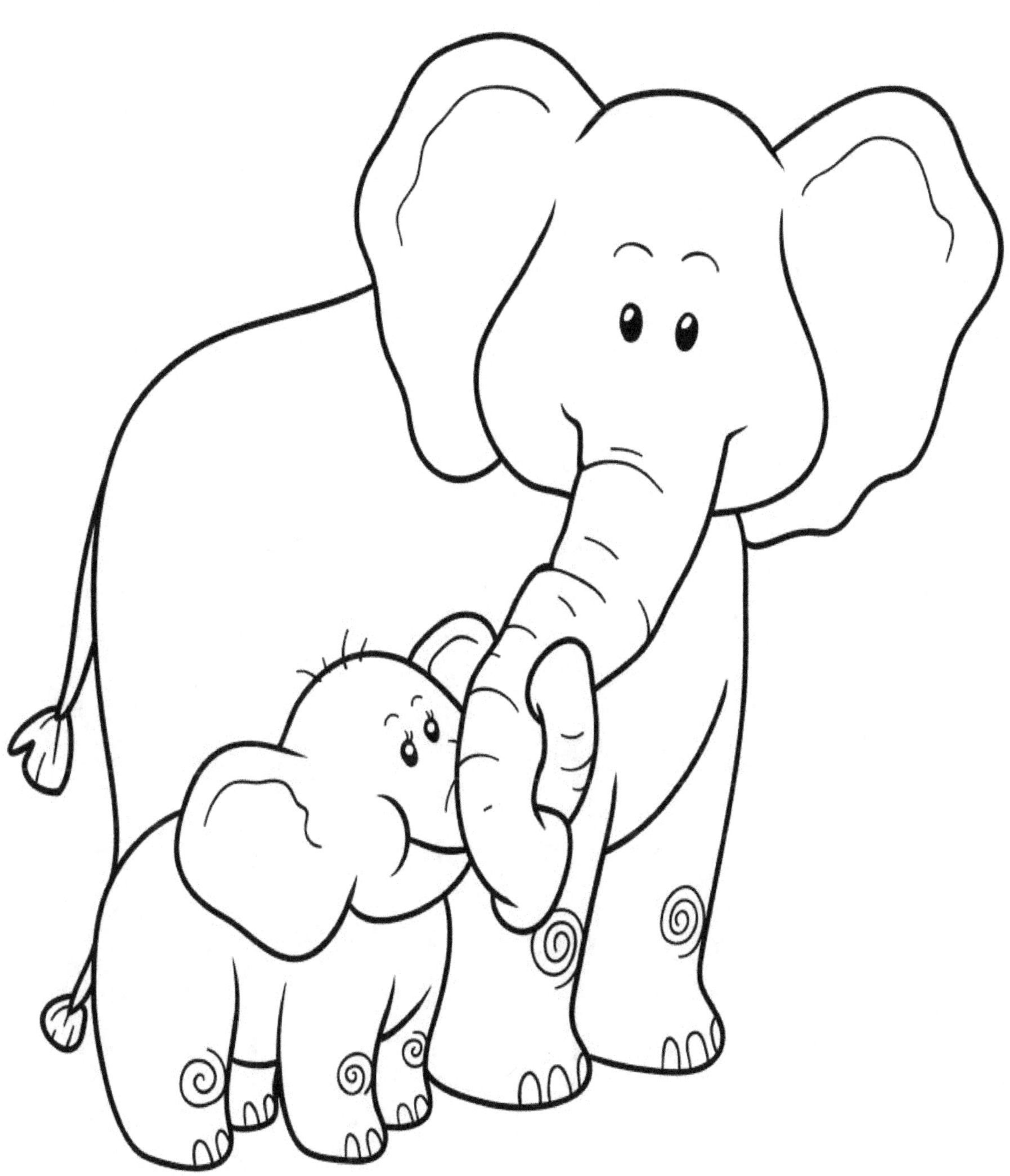

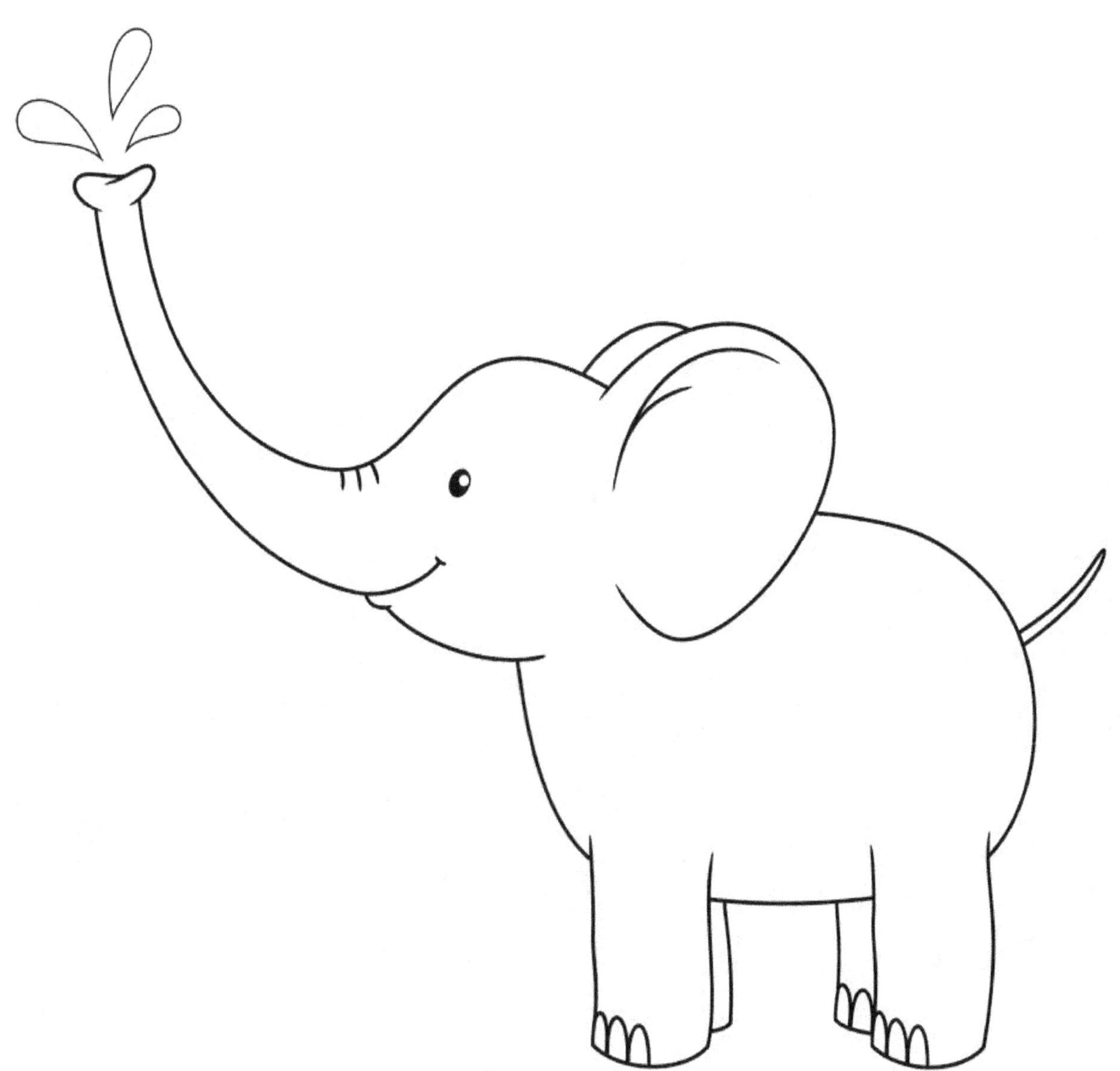

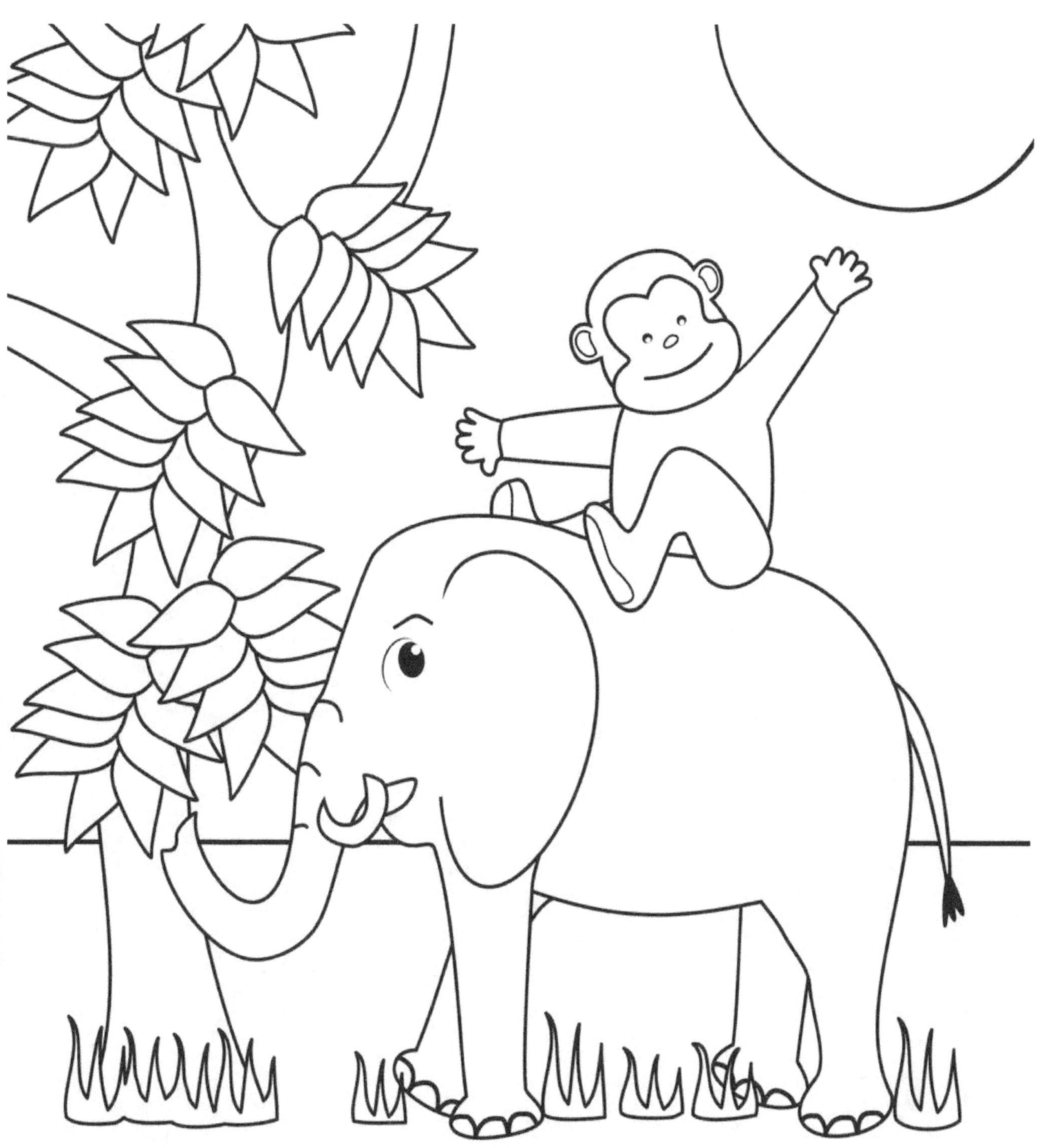

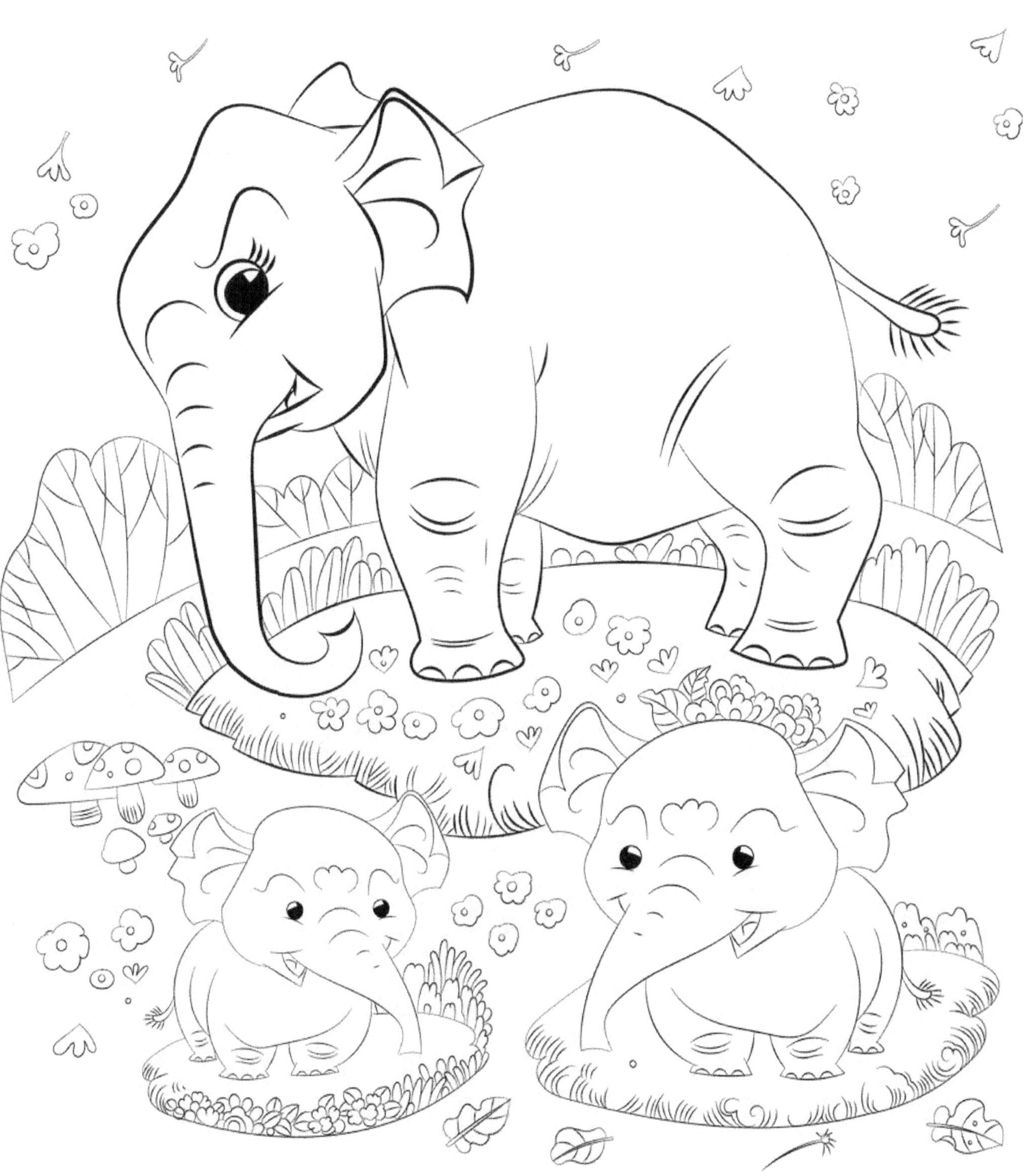

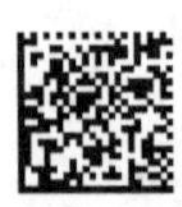
www.ingramcontent.com/pod-product-compliance
Lightning Source LLC
Chambersburg PA
CBHW081728250726
48657CB00010B/3184